IT'S ALL THE SAME TO ME

A Torah Guide To Inner Peace And Love Of Life

Moshe Gersht

"Thank you for your contribution to this field . . . Lots of gratitude for adding this contribution to the world's enlightenment."

Deepak Chopra, MD

"We live in a tumultuous time, with unprecedented stress. We are all desperate to find words of reassurance and comfort. Moshe Gersht has made us a great contribution with this book."

Abraham J. Twerski, author of *Angels Don't Leave Footprints*

"Spreading this wisdom in the world for others is freaking awesome. Whether people tune in to the universe for health, or wealth, or joy, *it's all the same to me.* I appreciate you being out there with the message."

Bob Doyle, featured in *The Secret*

"Moshe Gersht is sincere. It's a spiritual pleasure to engage with the wisdom of his mind and love of his heart."

David Aaron, author of *Love Is My Religion*

"Impacting, saving, helping, and enriching people's lives . . . A must read!"

Ryan Hollins, NBA Veteran and ESPN Sports Analyst

"Moshe Gersht presents a clear insight into the quality of mindful equanimity that can make all the difference between living in constant stress and living a serene life, no matter what the circumstances. Of course, this is easier said (or written) than done, but this book points the way."

Akiva Tatz, author of *Living Inspired*

"Although the concepts are intrinsically deep, it is presented in a manner that is easily understood. An effective means to gain a proper perspective that will enable one to live a happier, more productive, and more Torah-oriented life."

Zev Leff, Rabbinical Communal Leader

"The next level! The Power of Now meets The Power of Torah. Awesome guide to real inner work and exactly what the world needs right now.

Dov Ber Cohen, author of *Mastering Life*

Dedication

"And the years of Sarah's life were one hundred years, and twenty years, and seven years, were the years of her life." — Genesis 23:I

The famous commentator Rashi explains that the verse repeats the words "years of her life" to emphasize they were all equally good. But how could they have been considered equally good years? She spent most of her life barren, had relationship struggles, and was even kidnapped. But the truth is that when one understands that true happiness is not dependent on external circumstances, they can honestly say, "*It's all the same to me.*"

This book is dedicated to my zaidy and teacher, David "Donald" ben Bracha Kirsher *zatzuk"al*, may his soul elevate the cosmos.

—Shmuel Zacharias Menachem Mendel Maxx "pashut" HaCohen Herenstein, Rosh Yeshiva of Yeshivas Geulas Shaul

CONTENTS

Acknowledgments

Nothing happens on its own. This work, as well as everything else I have been blessed to accomplish or be a part of, is the fruit of many, and I have tremendous gratitude for everyone who has touched my life. First and foremost, I am grateful to God for all that I have been blessed with and for the guidance and clear loving Presence in my life. There is no amount of praise in the world that can do justice, and with that I humbly say, "Thank you."

To my wife, Avigial, my inspiration: You make the space for me to create, and you support everything I take on with authentic enthusiasm and see it as a new adventure. You are a gift and a partner in everything that comes through me. This journey is simply impossible without you. Thank you.

To my wonderful children, Chaviva, Ahava, and Akiva: You are joy incarnate. I love you so much. Thank you for giving me the opportunity to "walk the talk" and grow into the best person I am constantly becoming. Thank you for choosing me to be your guide.

To my parents, who have given me the tools, the love, and the space to evolve into who I am today: I am eternally grateful. Everything I do is an extension of your love in the world. Thank you.

To my brothers, Meir and Alex: Thank you for being the best brothers I could have ever chosen. One forever.

All of my in-laws, who have been the most supportive group a husband could ever ask for. Ta: I am inspired by your continual growth always, and my appreciation for everything you continue to do for my family is immense and beyond words. Thank you for being so supportive in every way and showing us what it means to be on a path of true growth.

Ma: Thank you for being our biggest fan, caring so deeply about us, and being by our side every step of the way. Your love is felt and appreciated. Naftali: You are a true gift. Thank you for always being on "Team Teddy." You are a true inspiration and I am so grateful for you. Yona, *chaviv sheli*: Thank you for your endless support, your constant smile, and your encouragement. None of this is possible without you. Annette, Tamar, Nomi, Ora, Zehava, Ephraim, Elisha, Shira, Yael, Menachem, Tehila, Ari, Gavriel, Mikka, Yishai, Shani, and Galya: It is a privilege to know you, and I am so grateful for everything you do, each in your own way. Yishai: Thank you for banging down my door, putting the Baal Shem Tov in front of me, and asking me to explain it to you. This book wouldn't have happened if not for you and your quest for truth.

To all of my teachers and guides who have been faithfully with me from the beginning of my journey: It is an honor to be your student and to have learned with and from you. What I teach is only a fraction of what I have gained from my time with you. My heart overflows with gratitude for everything you have shared with me.

In specific relation to this book project: Thank you, Rabbi Beryl Gershenfeld, Rav Asher Weiss, and Rav Doniel Katz for believing in me, supporting my aspirations, and always offering encouragement and wisdom. Thank you, Shula, for playing a central role in my journey. I can't describe my gratitude for everything you have placed before me. Thank you, Akiva, Nili, Meir, Binaymin, and Zev. Your insight during the last few years has helped shape me and how I live my life. Thank you, Shmuel. Your friendship means the world to me. Your constant encouragement and joy have filled this project with infinite light and positive energy. Thank you to all of my teachers who are no longer present but who are ever-present in my day-to-day life. For this work I want to specifically thank the Maharal, the Baal Shem Tov, Rebbe Nachman, and Dr. Wayne Dyer.

To Jon, Becky, Kenny, and Zach: Your energy and investment in my projects have never gone unnoticed. You have been exceedingly helpful in all that you do, and I have great appreciation for your time, energy, and effort. Thank you to everyone who read early copies of this book and gave me their thoughts and feedback.

Finally, I thank my great editors: Jessica Bryan and Adina Edelman. This work in its final form wouldn't exist without you. Avraham Kovel, thank you for your wisdom, patience, and help in creating this. You pushed me in order to pull out what you knew was there. I am so grateful. You are a partner in all who gain from its content.

Introduction

What's it all about? You know, life. It isn't just another question on the list of questions we can choose to ponder. It lies at the center of everything we do. The way you answer this question directly affects your behavior, your relationships, the way you think, and your belief system. The answer to this question determines your day-to-day motivation.

What I present to you in this book is a pointer toward the answer and is that which you already know somewhere deep within you. It is a reminder of that which has been forgotten somewhere along the way. The answer to this timeless question is buried within our collective consciousness and has been since time immemorial.

What we will discover together is that the most important thing you can bring to the world is your true self, with all its colors—not the image that has been created by your social network, nor the projected thoughts of your parents or friends. We will find that the most authentic version of yourself naturally has a positive disposition, and your joy will light up the room when you enter. Joy is your natural state. You don't have to chase after that which is already yours. All you need is to take off the gift wrapping and open the box you were given at birth.

JOY IS YOUR NATURAL STATE.

The essential teaching we will explore together is that although all things appear different on the surface, beneath the outward expression, there is buried a quality of "sameness" unifying all reality. It is this infinite light, expressed as an energy of love and spirit that flows through all of existence. By this I mean that even though we might appear different and have different lenses through which we experience life, beyond our differences we are connected. We are one. We are together.

What lies before you, then, is a choice. In every moment you can choose to put on another mask or take off an old layer. This is the deeper meaning behind the biblical words "Choose life." To live is to be attached to nothing other than what is real. And what is real? That which never changes.

There is an unchanging nature to who you are and to all that is. Will you take the surface layer of reality to be everything that exists—or accept that there is an energy flowing through all life that runs deeper than what you can see with your physical eyes? Are you open to discovering something that goes beyond ideas, something that is the truest experience possible? Throughout our youth, we pick up all sorts of negative beliefs. Are you willing to let go of these self-imposed limitations and allow yourself to open up to the idea of a love-filled universe that is working in your favor? These are the questions you need to ask if you truly want to experience life to its fullest.

What exactly is it that allows us to live life to its fullest? The answer is the degree of peace, joy, and love you experience at any given moment. It's only when we're at ease that life becomes weightless. It is only when we're in a state of joy that we enjoy the process of living. It is only when we feel love that we naturally want to give of ourselves to others. We're inspired to grow and channel this energy when we're plugged in. The goal of this book is to reawaken your own sense of inner peace so that you live with the high quality and positive energy you deserve.

It is in this peace that you will be able to breathe deeply and laugh fully. It is in this peace that you can hold space for someone you love. It is in this peace that you can express conviction without anger, strength without negativity, and confidence without arrogance. It is in this peace that you will be able to take on the world as it is, not as you wish it to be. In this peace you can face any situation with a high-quality "no" or an enthusiastic "yes."

We will discuss how to shift from a fragmented life in perpetual search for completion to a peace that extends love and creativity. They say you only live once, but this isn't quite true. You only die once, but you live anew every single day. How do you want to live each new day? Let it be in harmony with who you truly are.

THE DEGREE OF LOVE, JOY, AND PEACE YOU EXPERIENCE WILL DETERMINE THE QUALITY OF YOUR DOING IN ANY GIVEN MOMENT.

The ideas contained in this book are founded in two arenas. I have been blessed to invest the last decade and a half toward in-depth study and practice of Torah, Kabbalah, Chassidus, and Spirituality. The approach I have gleaned from these sources form the basis for how I see and map out the spiritual dimension. Through the years of service I pledged to the pages of great wisdom, I received inspiration and clarity from those who tread the path long before me. Nevertheless, ideas are only a starting point. My journey has been one of Divine clarity, followed by what some would call a *dark night of the soul,* which forced deep and rigorous contemplation. There were moments when I was so afraid of who I had become, the darkness of anger and depression, and the physical manifestations of my disrupted inner world. I felt as though I had lost myself and my Divine connection. And then, as though set free, I experienced liberation into clarity and love. Thus, the second pillar of this book is my personal experience of how these transformational ideas are not simply ideas but point to a truth that is beyond reason.

In the pages that follow, we will explore these questions through a lens of togetherness. I have chosen to write this book in two voices: the voice of the reader and the voice of the author. Written in question and answer form, I have attempted to hear the ideas being presented from the listener's perspective and then respond from the point I would like to present. This format also hints at the very nature of the discussion. Namely, sameness.

It's also worth noting that the first half of this book deals primarily with explaining the concepts in depth while the second half is primarily practical. As you read the pages, keep in mind that ideas will be more concretely described in later chapters. In addition, my suggestion in approaching this book is that you first read through its entirety to see the vision and feel the flow of ideas. The real work, however, begins when you subsequently go back and slowly digest the pages, concept by concept.

I sincerely hope that as we take this journey together, we can cultivate more clarity, and more importantly, find the peace and joy that is our birthright. The way into peace is to think about the question with which we began: What's it all about?

CHAPTER ONE

The Answer Is Love

The answer is love. The answer is you. The answer is underneath and inside. The answer is something beyond your analytical-thinking mind, and it has more to do with your essence than your present experience. The answer is something we often avoid because we are so stuck in our questions.

The ancient Aramaic etymology of the word "question," *kashia,* shares the same root as the word for straw, *kash.* Straw is the stalk that grains grow upon. The function of straw is to nourish the grain. However, straw has little to no nutritional value of its own. Imagine eating straw all your life instead of warm, nourishing bread. When we are stuck in questions, we lose the vital energy we need to fully embrace and appreciate life. If it helps you remember, think of it as getting *stuck* in the *stalk*. I want to address the question without getting stuck in the question. It is about seeing the answer.

TRADE IN THE QUESTION OF PAIN FOR THE ANSWER OF LOVE.

Underlying our mutual emotional struggles is the question of *why*. *Why is this happening to me? Why aren't you listening to me? Why did that happen to him or her? Why aren't you being fair? Why weren't they honest with me? Why did I get a traffic ticket?* Behind these questions, there is judgment about a life situation, which creates a negative charge or resistance. We assume none of these things should be happening. Is this normal? Yes.

We all have the propensity for these negative judgements. We are born and raised to judge, assess, and evaluate situations. This is how the mind works. It's a very good thing too. We need the ability to assess situations in order to make good decisions. Without this ability we wouldn't stop at a red light, choose to eat healthy, or walk away from a toxic relationship. However, problems begin to arise the moment we turn our assessment into a story that creates pain—or in other words, dramatize our life situation. Instead of living in the moment, we mentally (and sometimes verbally) write a dramatic narrative that creates, surrounds, and concretizes our pain and perpetuates the unrest we experience.

This pain is negative energy or *negativity* that moves you further away from happiness. Further away from Truth. Further away from Love. Further away from God. In this sense, we are all born as equals. We are the same in our innate human challenge, which is our inability to see things as they are behind the veil of appearance.

The same negativity starts every war, from the small argument with a brother, sister, or friend to the genocides and holocausts throughout history. All negativity comes from the same place. The same source.

What is the source of negativity? What is the source of life's dramas?

The drama in our lives is created through the way we experience whatever happens to us: the way we judge what people say to us, the judgments we make about ourselves, and the way we perceive all the situations and conditions we find ourselves in. It's not the situation that creates the person, or the feeling within the person, but rather the way we view life that creates our sense of the situations we encounter.

HOW YOU SEE IS MORE IMPORTANT THAN *WHAT* YOU SEE.

This may bring up the question about objective good and negative situations. Later in this book, we will discuss the difference between good and bad. However, in the meantime I ask that you suspend your thoughts about the question of good and evil and instead come with me on a journey to discover whether there is another way of looking at things.

The answer begins with *Hishtavus*. The answer is *now*.

What does Hishtavus mean, and why is it important?

Hishtavus is related to the word *Shaveh,* which literally means "the same." Thus, meaning "sameness," "Oneness," or "equanimity," Hishtavus is a state of nonjudgmental awareness. You are able to totally accept reality as it is without labeling things as essentially better or worse.[1] It is the beginning of what it means to live in the presence of God. It is the secret of life.

The Baal Shem Tov, known as the founder of Chassidus, describes this sameness as being the fundamental principle upon which all of spiritual development rests. The twelfth-century Spanish philosopher Bahya ibn Paquda writes, in his famous work *Duties of the Heart,* that Hishtavus is the most important spiritual practice and quality one can attain.

---

[1] Rav Moshe Iserles begins his editorial notes of the Shulchan Aruch with the Psalm "*I place God before me always*" and says that this is the fundamental principle of Torah and the essential quality of what makes the righteous, righteous. The Hebrew word for *I place* is *Shivisi,* which shares the same etymological root as *Shaveh,* which means equal or the same. Thus the fundamental ideal in living a spiritual life is sameness. It is noteworthy that the famous Kabbalists the Arizal and Rav Moshe Dovid Volle all understood this verse the same way.

You can live in harmony with all of life and enter into conscious alignment with a higher order. This state of allowing and surrender opens a space inside of you that engenders renewed creativity, connection, and the experience of love to expand. Seeing life through this lens of Oneness lets you see the good and the love laced within creation. There are seven life-changing qualities related to sameness. Harmony, alignment with a higher order, love recognition, allowing, surrender, space, and a lens of Oneness. Let me explain.

Hishtavus means to live in perfect harmony with all of life. Life is happening. It stops for no one. It has been said that life is God in action. When Moshe (Moses) asked God, "Who shall I tell the people is setting them free from Egyptian bondage?" God responded with the words, "*Ekyeh Asher Ekyeh,*" "I am that I am" or "I will be Who I will be." Things *are* as they *are.* They will be as they will be. To live in the denial of this truth is to deny the presence of God. To live in harmony with this truth is to live in the presence of God.

Hishtavus is to enter into conscious alignment with a higher order. There is a deeper intention behind everything that occurs. Nothing ends with what we see on the surface. There is always more behind the scenes. The Creator, Sustainer, and Director of life, as it unfolds, has intentions of the highest good and love. We only see a small fraction of reality. Being open to this spiritual guidance allows for openness in all our experiences, with the people we meet and the places we go. Living with equanimity, you will find a hidden harmony, a sacredness, a higher order in which the knowing, the known, and the knower are one. It is the fertile ground for wisdom and freedom and a space for compassion and love. True sameness produces radiance and warmth of being. There is an ease within that comes when we see a bigger picture. It is being able to hold space for unlimited potential and infinite possibility—an inner knowing that all things lead in the right direction, whether or not it unfolds according to how we think it should.

Hishtavus is recognizing the love that exists everywhere. It is the awareness that the energy of all things and events are flooded with a loving presence of the Creator, despite their outer appearance. It is possible to literally feel the connection between you and all other creations, all part of the love story being told by God. You are totally conscious of the miracle of life and see how love is the epicenter of creation.

Hishtavus is a state of allowing. To allow things to happen with inner resistance is not weakness. It is strength. Non-resistance doesn't mean letting people walk all over you or allowing your house to burn down. Whatever is happening, instead of wishing it were different, you allow it to be exactly as it is, then take action from that place of allowing.

Hishtavus is a state of surrender. Although we associate the word *surrender* with a negative charge or loss, surrender is a powerful door opener for peace, love, and harmony. We seem to constantly be in a fight with reality. There's never enough time, not enough money, and we're always doing the things we wish we weren't doing. But to surrender means to let go of how you think things *should* be and accept them as how they *are*.

Hishtavus is a space inside us that allows creativity, connection, and love to expand. Connection and flow happen within the space of sameness. It is not a form of doing. It is a space, an inner stillness that allows for and fosters authentic connection. It is the silence out of which a song is born, the quiet from which breakthroughs and epiphanies emerge.

Hishtavus is seeing life through the lens of Oneness. According to Kabbalah, there are five levels of consciousness, the highest being *yechida* – Oneness. Instead of seeing division, we see unity. Instead of separation, we see togetherness. Instead of difference, sameness. It is an all-inclusive way of viewing the world.

It does not mean repressing our emotions. It can be easy to confuse sameness with denial, but it is not about denying a particular situation. Rather, it is about accepting each situation for what it is and dropping all resistance. Denial means looking into the face of reality and covering it up with a label that says something to the effect that, "Everything is okay. Don't get angry." Denial leads to more pain, while *Hishtavus* leads the way to freedom.

It doesn't mean you always feel amazing. It might seem that if we're at peace with everything that happens, we will always feel fantastic, but this isn't the promise of sameness. On the outer layer of reality, i.e., life as we know it, things are always changing. Nothing stays the same, nothing lasts forever, and nothing is everything it seems. Because of the nature of life, there are things we experience that make us very happy and things that make us sad. This is how it's supposed to be. The only difference is that with sameness, these remain on the surface, while behind them you rest in a deep sense of peace, presence, and love that is unshakable.

I deeply appreciate the way Rav Doniel Katz defines equanimity as "the capacity to maintain an open, connected state, free from emotional turbulence, no matter what daily chaos and challenges you face." Dr. Judith Orloff describes this in two words in her book's title, *Emotional Freedom*.

LIFE IS GOD IN ACTION.

BEING IN HARMONY WITH LIFE ALLOWS YOU TO SEE LOVE AND OPPORTUNITY EVERYWHERE.

What you will find is that equanimity allows you to remain centered in the middle of whatever is happening. It gives you balance, strength, and stability. This stillness is a deep presence of inner calm, well-being, confidence, vitality, and integrity. It keeps us upright in the same way a ballast keeps a ship upright in strong winds. This is an invitation of freedom sowing its seeds. Water it and allow it to grow.

Simply put:

All is equal.

It is all the same.

All is one.

All is good.

And all is love.

There is no difference. There is no separation.

Something to ask yourself is whether or not these seven qualities resonate within you as something you have personally experienced. If you have, what was the catalyst? If you have not, can you imagine what might be holding you back? Are there times when you feel rooted in something so strong that you stay firmly planted when the winds of the world blow? The most important book to study is the journal of your heart.

CHAPTER TWO

The Secret Switch

Can you be a little more practical? What is it like to live with sameness?

Sure. Practically, sameness means living with an inner "yes." Through cultivating this attitude of nonattachment and nonresistance, you feel more confident in everything you do. When I say living with an inner yes, I mean that no matter what shows up for you in your life, instead of fighting it, you choose to say yes to what is happening.

For example: You would like to get to a meeting on time. You leave your house early, take a short cut, and nevertheless find yourself in a traffic jam. You become immediately aware that you are going to be at least fifteen minutes late. Your inner "no" to the situation causes you to get upset and frustrated for the next half hour as you mentally shout about how angry you are at the situation.

Equanimity says "yes." It need not be an enthusiastic or excited yes. Just yes. A simple inner *Yes, this is what's happening now* can totally transform your life. Imagine if instead of getting frustrated by the stop-and-go traffic, you fully accepted it as an opportunity to listen to the podcast you've been pushing off listening to, or you call your cousin whom you haven't spoken to in ages. With a different lens, you may experience that life has just presented you with a gift. Instead of wasting precious energy getting "stuck in the stalk," you are already in the grain of your day. You can choose to see life situations as assignments that have shown up for you. Instead of resisting and creating negative energy, accept and even embrace what happens in a way that allows you to be at peace. Not only will you feel better, but you will make better decisions in the moments that follow.

Let's say you did get angry during that car ride. What kind of person are you going to be on the phone if you call someone? What are you going to be feeling when you finally arrive at your destination? In fact, what good did it do to get angry at all? Did it change the situation?

Ask yourself: Why was I so anxious over being late? Why was I upset when I lost my job?

LIVE WITH AN INNER YES TO LIFE
AND LIFE WILL BE SAYING YES TO YOU.

There are no problems, only situations. What do I mean? A problem is a concept that we create in our mind; we decide something isn't good, and thus it is a problem. Problems come with excessive stress, anxiety, sadness, and fear. It is very easy for us to turn situations into problems.

Usually, however, you will discover that what you define as a problem is actually anything that doesn't go according to your plans. You believe something has gone against your desire. It is when something you don't want to happen has taken place, or you feel the anxiety of it potentially happening in the future. These are what we have universally decided to call "problems."

When we see things from the lens of separation—meaning we have a subjective definition of better or worse—there can be little to no acceptance of what is happening. In its place there will be resistance, resentment, frustration, anger, and irritation.

Instead of creating more problems, we can choose to see what is happening without the label. You can decide that as an alternative to waging war with life, you can wage peace with yourself. Choose to see reality, feel the feelings that come with the reality, and accept it. With this comes a peace from which you can choose to do something about the situation that has presented itself.

Are you saying that I shouldn't want anything?

No. The problem is we don't know how to want. We have never learned how to properly want anything. We just assumed we knew how and have lived our lives as if we didn't need training in our wanting.

There is something I call "resistant wanting." This type of wanting comes with a label attached that reads, "If I get what I want, it is good, and I am happy. If I don't get what I want, it is bad, and I am unhappy." Psalms 55:23 says, "Throw the load you carry onto God, and He will take care of you." What load are you carrying? What is the heavy baggage weighing you down that you take with you everywhere you go? It is the resistant wanting, your desire that defines what is good or bad. It is this resistance and judgment that is the burden you carry. Throw it up to God and know that the highest good will unfold. *God will take care of you* means that when you can let go of your plans, your desires, and your thoughts and opinions about life as being absolute, you will be free of your heavy burden.

Then there is "surrendered wanting," which is your ability to be enthusiastic and desire something without being attached to the outcome. You are thus able to have an opinion but also maintain an open mind and accept you might not know the whole picture. Surrender is not about giving up, but about giving over. It is going for what you love and appreciating the process and enjoying the success if it comes. In the same breath, it also means embracing failure because you see it as part of a bigger success.

The goal is not to do nothing, nor is it to desire nothing. The goal is not to avoid thinking, nor is it to be nothing. The goal is to let go of the smallness inside you that keeps you trapped in the valueless opinions of your ego. This letting go will allow you to step into your greatness as part of the infinite and hold hands with destiny as you walk through life. Surrendered wanting is to let go of how you think things should be and follow the spiritual guidance that is always being sent to you. I am touched by the way Gabrielle Bernstein expresses this in her book *The Universe Has Your Back*:

> When you humbly surrender, you begin to receive guidance far beyond your physical sight. Often you'll feel a presence within you and around you, guiding your thoughts and feelings. Don't be afraid to dive deeply into the infinite pool of inner wisdom that is available to you now. Open your heart and mind to new perceptions. Allow yourself to surrender to the flow of love that always guides you.

The Ethics of Our Fathers states, "Make His will your will, so that He can make your will His will." The sages understood that when you align your desire with what is actually happening, your life will begin to unfold in a way that *truly* fulfills desire.

Live as if you have chosen whatever you feel or experience at this moment. This is really the seat of your free will. Your choice begins with how you view your life. No outcomes are yours and all outcomes are good. In this lies the peace of God.

LIVE AS IF YOU HAVE CHOSEN YOUR CIRCUMSTANCES. INSTEAD OF ASKING WHY, START ASKING, WHAT CAN I LEARN FROM THIS?

To summarize these points:

- Surrendered wanting doesn't mean avoid trying. It means to try without being attached to outcomes.

- It does not mean avoid doing anything. It means do everything you can without thinking you're in control of the results.

- It does not mean to avoid thinking. It means to think without fooling yourself that you know the whole picture.

- It does not mean thinking of yourself as nothing. It means knowing you are part of the everything-ness that is life, and you are never separate.

We all tend to hold on tightly to that which we believe we must control. But as a point of self-inquiry, investigate where in your life you are still holding on to something you might benefit from surrendering to a higher order. The answer to this question might contain a portal to deeper peace in your total experience.

SURRENDER IS NOT ABOUT GIVING UP. IT'S ABOUT GIVING OVER.

So are you saying that nothing matters?

No. I would not phrase it that way. These are the things that must not matter to you:

1. What happens.

2. What people think of you.

3. What you have and what you don't.

4. Your spiritual level and the things that block you from growth.

So then, what does matter?

Everything . . . Everything matters. Nothing can be miscounted.

Everything does matter, just not in the way you think it does. Things matter in that everything happens for a deeper reason and fits perfectly into the Creator's masterpiece of life. However, your opinion and judgment of a situation don't matter, in that they're often incorrect and biased by your limitations. When you label something as good or bad, that has no bearing on the reality of the situation. What you think about a situation may matter to you, but it only matters in a relative sense and not in an absolute sense.

We see things through our limitations and beliefs that were handed to us by other human beings and our own subjective experience of life. Thus, we're almost always going to be seeing things without total vision and will come to misunderstand reality. Therefore, when I say that your perspective doesn't matter, what I really mean to say is that the way you see things does not include the whole picture. How do I know? Because if you saw the whole picture, nothing would ever contradict the way you see things. But the reality is that some situations are the opposite of how you thought they *should* be. You can ask yourself, "How often is the word *should* causing me pain and creating my problems?" Nobody plans for a global pandemic. Nobody plans for a flat tire. There is a part inside of me that immediately thinks, *This isn't supposed to happen. This is my problem.* The truth is, if there is a problem, it's because in that moment I am not walking with God. I have temporarily forgotten what it means to be in this world. When you lose your stillness, you lose touch with your inner self. When you lose touch with your inner self, you can lose yourself in the world.

This is not fatalism. It is freedom.

EVERYTHING MATTERS. JUST NOT IN THE WAY YOU THINK IT DOES.

We create, sustain, and direct our own pain through our attachment to fear and our desires. We can also create, sustain, and direct our joy and peace through letting go and moving back into harmony with our higher selves. This choice is what it means to be made in the image of God.

The Psalmist writes, *"Happy are the people that for them this is so."* What a powerful thought that can change your entire perspective. *This is so.* Can we live with *this is so?* The happy ones are those who can live and be at peace with an attitude of *this is* so. They have learned to let go and flow. This is sameness.

CHAPTER THREE

Setting Down Your Mind

So is this all just a mindset?

It's more than a mindset. It's setting the mind down and taking a rest. Use the mind for what it's good at: thinking, analyzing, developing ideas, contemplation, and the like, but know that when you see your convictions—your thoughts, opinions, and beliefs—as being the only way, then it's time to wake up and realize that you're no longer using the tool that is your mind; it's using you. That's when it's time to set the mind down and tap into your higher consciousness.

**Are you telling me that I should put down my beliefs and dreams of
what I want to accomplish in my life?**

No. When I say you should put your mind down, I mean
you should put your ego down.

Yes, be passionate about what you believe. Yes, do
everything you can to pursue your dreams. However, you might
notice that when you're passionate, you have a tendency to think
you're the sole owner of the truth and *need* things to happen a
certain way. Do not for a moment think that you are the decider
of what is good or bad, what should or shouldn't happen, and
that if you are proven wrong, you have wasted time or energy.
You have done exactly what you were supposed to do. I spent
over seven years pursuing a career as the lead singer in a rock
band. In the end, it appears, being the front man of a pop-punk
band is not my essential mission in this world. But does that
mean that all the years of time, energy, and money invested in
this dream were wasted? Absolutely not. They were all stepping
stones and bridges that led me to where I am today. I learned
lessons and garnered skills and abilities I may never have
otherwise developed. Even when that dream ended, there was no
room for negativity. The goal is always to continue building and

developing without adding negative energy to the process. Negativity can only generate more pain and frustration.

Stop creating more pain for yourself by resisting *what is*— as in wanting to be someone else, be somewhere else, or doing something else. Resistance only increases the drama in our lives. Surrender will end the drama in your life. It won't stop life from happening, but the story we attach to it will fall by the wayside. Goodbye, drama.

Pause and reflect on where you are still resisting what is already happening. Understand that resistance leads to resentment. Resentment leads to pain. To alleviate undesirable and unnecessary discomfort in your life, see where you can lean in and yield to what is happening instead of protesting.

WHEN WE LET GO OF RESISTANCE AND STEP INTO ACCEPTANCE, WE RECEIVE NEW SOLUTIONS INSTEAD OF OLD PROBLEMS.

Instead of having arguments, you will have discussions. You'll be able to make your points firmly and clearly without expressing any reactive or defensive energy.

Instead of beating up on yourself for messing up, you'll accept that mistakes happen. You'll be able to fully value who you are and know your worthiness despite making errors in judgment. We are perfectly imperfect. We're not supposed to be anybody else.

Negativity is only a mindset. It is an illusion. All the different "problems" of your life—the things that appear to be opposite, different, and against—are a secondary truth; they are not ultimate reality. This vision is broken off from the bigger whole. It offers an incomplete picture. All resistance is negativity in some form or another. The things that seem to be *going wrong* are exactly as they are supposed to be. How do I know? Because they are happening.

The reason we view them as problems, according to Rebbe Nachman of Breslov, is because we are distant from Oneness. Negativity and resistance arise because we are living in separation, because we see our thoughts and ourselves as separate from the mind of God, and because we are separate from the Divine order.

King David said, *"I shall place God before me always."* What this really means is that whenever I see something that appears to be standing before me, in front of me, blocking me, or against me—i.e., it looks like a problem—this is where I shall place God. This is where I shall place the idea of a bigger picture. A unified reality of love and purpose. I will remind myself that there is no opposition when we are dealing with Oneness. Thus I replace this experience with a knowing that everything stems from One source, from God.

Life is not working against me; it's working for me. It's not an enemy; it's a friend. It's not different; it's the same. Trade in your resistance for acceptance and your pain for peace; trade your problems for the ultimate solution. Life is not happening to you. It's happening for you.

I'm getting a better understanding, but please give me a few more examples.

Of course. One of the most basic things that throws us off-kilter is what other people think about us. When they think we are wise and even praise us, we feel we are worthy and have done something well. When they think we are dumb and let us know it, we feel upset and start to question our own value. But why does it matter what other people think of you? Their judgments are simply that. *Their* judgments. *Their* opinion. It has absolutely nothing to do with the essence of who you are.

In the state of equanimity, your feelings about yourself and your feelings about others don't change because they have an opinion. Just the opposite happens. Being aware of the judgments and labels of others keeps you awake to the Truth. They are the little reminders, the subtle alarm clocks that keep us awake. Use the judgments of others to keep you on your toes without buying into what they think. Let it be the same to you whether or not people think you know everything or know nothing. Through this you are One with God.

Let it be all the same to you. Whether people think you know nothing or everything is irrelevant. You belong to a higher order of living where opinions and judgments don't matter.

LET IT BE THE SAME TO YOU WHETHER PEOPLE THINK YOU KNOW EVERYTHING OR KNOW NOTHING AT ALL.

Here is another view. In his book *You Can Be Happy No Matter What,* Dr. Richard Carslon uses the metaphor of someone coming into a room and throwing a ball at you. Naturally, you throw up your hands to catch the ball. It's instinctual. You catch the ball to protect yourself. We do the same thing with insults, blame, and criticism. We stand up to defend ourselves. Someone comes into the room, and they are upset about something, so they throw their energy at you with their words. But when it comes to negative energy, you never have to catch someone else's "ball." You can let it fall to the ground at your feet.

You might find it helpful to have a few go-to sentences in your back pocket that you can deploy to help deflate the tension of a given situation in order to help this ball drop. *Is that so? Really? Tell me more. Let me think about that. I could totally see how this bothers you.* In responding this way, you have shown your willingness to hear the person who is in pain without taking in the emotional charge they are throwing at you.

Or if it helps, you can imagine yourself as being transparent to the thoughts and words of others and let the words pass through you, offering no resistance. See how it feels to live without the need to catch someone else's ball. In this sense, the presence is the power of observation, the ability to see without being caught by what we see. When well-developed, such power gives rise to a great sense of peace. This is something you can learn to carry with you everywhere you go.

But what about physical pain? I can't just turn off my body sensing that it really hurts. I really don't want to be in pain.

The Maharal of Prague wrote, "Although the righteous does in fact feel pain, he does not suffer." What he means with these words is that pain is a part of life. It is not something you can avoid or escape. In fact, many people see sameness as a way to escape the pain of life, but Hishtavus is not about escape at all. It is deeply embracing and loving all of life. We move deeper into life, rather than away from our present reality.

When you are feeling pain, and we all feel pain, be there fully with the pain. Cry when you feel like crying. Breathe deeply into the throbbing of a headache until it passes. Be *in* pain with grace, instead of resentfully wishing the pain would stop. Don't fight yourself. The resistance turns pain into a problem and thus into suffering. Embracing the pain doesn't make the pain go away, but it stops the pain from being a problem.

Does this mean I shouldn't try to stop or avoid pain?

No. Of course you should take action whenever possible. If there is a way to alleviate the pain, by all means do what is good for your body. The idea here is that anytime you are wishing you were somewhere else, in some other body or in some other time, you are further generating suffering for your heart. You are denying the truth about what is. Instead, accept and be in harmony with what is. Live with an attitude of *I am what I am; I will be what I will be.*

But isn't it good to dream of a better time? What about manifesting myself into better health?

Yes. Of course. Dream and dream daily. It is one of the most powerful practices. But first you must be still. Then you can dream. Here we are discussing the moments of pain when dreaming is not possible and all you can do is focus on the pain. In these moments, the way forward is to be fully present with our pain, emotional or physical. The serenity prayer of the twelve-steps program was formed with this in mind:

God, grant me the serenity to accept the things I cannot change, the courage to change the things I can, and the wisdom to know the difference.

CHAPTER FOUR

You're Not Who You Think You Are

I have always used the word "ego" to mean arrogant or full of myself. How do you use the word "ego"?

The verse in Deuteronomy says, "And it is I that stands in between you and God." Although the verse itself is speaking about Moshe, the deeper meaning of the verse alludes to the fact that the "I" (what we call the "ego") stands between you and all that is true.

The great sage known as the Alter of Kelm would say, "In the beginning there was one voice. Then there were two. Now there is one. Our first step is to at the very least return back to hearing two voices." What he meant was this: In the beginning of our lives, there is only the voice of our soul. The voice of our conscience. Then, as we develop, we gain a second voice: the voice of our ego. The Torah refers to this voice as the *Yetzer Hara*. As we develop further, we lose touch with the sound of our soul, and all that's left is the one voice, the voice of our ego. Our job is to start recognizing that there are two voices. This is the first step on the journey home.

In this regard, the ego is your false sense of self. It's when you experience yourself as merely a body that can feel and think, and nothing more. It is the sense of being disconnected from everything in reality, including God. In the ego state, you believe you are only the sum total of the story of your life; the events you experience, your personality, your social networks, and your talents or the lack thereof. But this isn't the whole truth. It's only a very small fraction of who you are. Most of who you are is not even in your body.

Yetzer Hara literally means "the creative force that is undeveloped; an immature perspective." Relating to life in this constricted way, it gives us a false perception of reality. It is the same way a child doesn't understand why eating candy all day is bad or that wearing a seatbelt is good. As long as you continue thinking in this small and narrow way, you will likely continue to choose short-term pleasures over long-term pleasures. The more identified you are with this voice, the more you will naturally avoid anything that could indicate the voice is wrong. In this regard, the ego will do everything in its power to keep you distracted from what's truly important. Think about it like this. If you were to prove this old perspective wrong, that would mean its death. When you identify with the ego, there is a part of you that fears your own ego death. The ego recognizes this threat, and in your subconscious, works very hard at sidetracking you from the Truth.

RECOGNIZING THE VOICE OF THE EGO IS THE FIRST STEP ON YOUR JOURNEY HOME.

In his book *The Power of Intention,* Dr. Wayne Dyer says there are six main characteristics of the ego. The ego believes I am what I have; I am what I do; I am what others think of me; I am separate from everyone; I am separate from everything missing in my life; and, most importantly, I am separate from

God. Ego is simply an idea of who you are that you carry around with you. You can either choose to be a hostage to your ego or a host to God. This is the seat of your free will. Free will means you have the choice to connect to spirit or not.

Basically, your ego is your set of opinions, biases, desires, and fears, all of which are born out of your life experiences. You take all these things to be true facts, but the truth is they are just a very small perspective of a very big reality.

What's an example of how the Ego runs my life?

Take expectations, as an example. Your expectations are actually your subconscious ego desires. They are the "shoulds" of your life. However, expectations do not serve you. Expectations are resentments waiting to happen. The only thing you can expect for sure is that the outer layer of your life experiences will always be changing. When you can learn to drop your expectations and embrace deep acceptance and gratitude, you will find that joy and more energy will flow into you and your life.

Expectations take the infinite potential of the future and form a picture of what it should be. Instead of experiencing the wonder of what might flower into being in the forthcoming present, you are trapped in a vision of what you think your reality should be. In doing this, you create resistance to any other possibilities and create more pain and suffering for yourself and others. This is how the ego works. It has been said the ego stands for "**E**dging **G**od **O**ut." When you think you understand the whole picture on your own, you've made the decision that you know better than God regarding how things should develop. You forget that there is an intention behind all things in life, and this intention is for your highest good. Not only that, but you open yourself up for major disappointment.

We are all raised to live with expectations. Therefore, it's not uncommon to live with expectations, and it's perfectly natural to have them. Nevertheless, your life without them engenders more peace. The question becomes whether you choose to maintain the way you've viewed reality your whole life or decide to let go of undesirable perspectives.

EXPECTATIONS ARE RESENTMENTS WAITING TO HAPPEN

I understand the value of dropping expectations, but I still feel like it is ok to want things to be a certain way. I want many things in life. Is there anything wrong with wanting?

Think about this for a moment: Why do you *want* most of the things you want? Because you want to *feel* a certain way. We all want to feel safe, secure, and taken care of. We want to feel love, joy, and connection. We want to feel valuable, worthy, and good. We want to feel authentic, genuine, and kind. This is what we call "wholeness." At the deeper level, this is what we call "holiness." But at some level, we feel like we're missing something. We're lacking in some way. Part of us feels like something is wrong and there is a problem. Sometimes this is expressed as a feeling of not being good enough, shame, inauthenticity, sadness, anger, frustration, depression, feeling alone, weak, scared, or altogether lacking or empty. As a result, our desire for more wholeness increases.

So then what happens? We attempt to fill the void with things or satiate our desire with a *change of identity*. We grab onto material things, wealth, social status and power, relationships, physical pleasure, and new experiences. But inevitably we fail and fall back to square one, or we achieve our goals and grieve because we still feel like we are missing something. Not long afterward, we will be back on "our search for wholeness."

This is how most of us go through most of life, most of the time.

For many, the pain becomes so great that we develop addictions, obsessions, and other psychological challenges such as depression and anxiety. People will go to great lengths to numb the pain, quiet the fear, and feed the desire. This is the ego—the Yetzer Hara—the undeveloped perspective (and consequently desire) to look for wholeness in the wrong places.

Why do we get so stuck in this pointless cycle? We have a distorted view of reality in which we think wholeness is *if-there-then: If* things are different, when I get *there,* and when it's not now but *then.* We are addicted to the past and the future—the good old days and the dream life. The truth is that all "problems" are spiritual in nature—whatever you are struggling with is a *symptom* of the real problem.

It looks something like this:

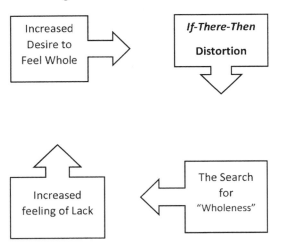

We end up taking the wrong turn away from Truth and detour into falsehood. Many of us end up stuck in this vicious cycle for most or all of our lives. However, some of us become so broken by the cycle that, often through trauma, we are given Divine direction onto the path of enlightenment. After looking for love in all the wrong places, we realize it's already right where we are.

You may find it useful to study your own personal *if-there-then distortion* so you can begin to notice when it creeps into your decision making. What do you believe is going to give you what you don't already have?

This is a pretty novel thought. Wouldn't you say it's good to be striving for something great in your life?

There is nothing wrong with striving, except for the fact that you may never be arriving. People like to ask, "What would you do today if you knew you would die tomorrow?" Another way to approach this might be to ask yourself: *What if I had everything I want today? What would I do if all my desires were fulfilled? Who would I be if all my fears were removed? What would be left of me if I achieved all the success I desire and had nothing to be afraid of?* I suggest you take a few minutes to pause and ask yourself these questions. This could be one of the most important exercises you will ever do. The answer to these questions will point you in the direction of your true self, right now.

The Talmud says: "What should a person do if they want to live? Kill yourself." No, they were not encouraging suicide. They were talking about the ego that you are convinced is you; kill your false sense of self. Rabbeinu Jonah Gerondi described this in his classic *Gates of Return* as the ability to "die before you die." This is the way to freedom. This is the true meaning of the words self-sacrifice. Renounce the ego and pledge allegiance to your soul.

Ego is invested with bias and opinion. Experiencing sameness removes this bias. Instead of having a personal prejudice—being in favor of or against—you can allow things to be as they are while strive rg to align your will with something that runs deeper than opinion. Abandon favoring and opposing and develop complete openness to experience, without being lost in reactions of like and dislike. Only once we've given up our biases can we experience life without being hooked by either desire or aversion.

ABANDON YOUR NEED FOR THINGS TO BE THE WAY YOU THINK THEY ARE SUPPOSED TO BE. IT IS THE ATTACHMENT TO A FALSE REALITY THAT PERPETUATES PAIN AND FRUSTRATION.

I'm not talking about indifference. Quite the contrary. I am describing a life so fully engaged with the love embedded within reality that we don't give negativity or popular opinion our focus and attention. This knowing is already deeply embedded within our consciousness. It is what spiritualists and religions have been describing throughout history as the "soul." This is what King Solomon meant when he said, "God made people straight, but they engaged in excessive thinking." Our nature is healthy, holy, and aligned with something profoundly simple. We overcomplicate our lives by developing opinions based on our relative experiences. Carlos Castaneda said it like this: "Man has given up silent knowledge for the world of reason."

This simplicity and lack of ego investment define the core of humility. When you think of someone who exudes humbleness, what stands out is not that they think they are worthless or that they are constantly praising others. It's that they seem to see themselves as no better or no worse than anybody else. They see through the lens of sameness. They might even be some of the greatest leaders, artists, and influencers of a generation, but they recognize that the power they have is not of their own and doesn't belong to them.

They know we are all made equal in the image of God, we are the same, and we are all equally powerful in our ability to shine light in the world. Gary Zukav, in *The Seat of the Soul*, eloquently says, "You are only as powerful as that for which you stand." When you stand for your own ego, you only have the power of an individual splintered off from the rest of humanity. However, when you stand for the wholeness of life, you are endowed with the collective power of life. As we've mentioned, Hishtavus comes from the word *Shaveh,* which literally means "the same." Ego is the exact opposite. Ego finds separation. Ego sees difference. The truth of who you are sees love, connection, and unity.

I was often bothered by an apparent contradiction. On the one hand, we are made in the image of God. On the other hand, we are but the dust of the earth. Which one is it? All powerful or absolutely nothing? The answer lies beneath the two. We are made in the image of God, but like the dust of the earth, we are all the same. We might have different roles in creation in the same way a rock is not a tree or a cat, but we all share something in common: we each reveal different colors of the same light.

Sameness and humility are inseparable. Humility is the realization that there is no difference between you and the dust of the earth, and yet you are made in the image of God and filled with the light of the Infinite. To be humble is not to think of yourself as nothing but to realize that you are everything and no different than everything else in the world.

A practice I believe you will enjoy is to make a list of several people you may find offensive or don't get along with. Notice the feeling you have inside of yourself when you think of their name and image. Afterward, next to each name, write down all the things you have in common with them. Put all your energy and attention on the sameness you share. When you are finished, wish them a silent blessing. Check back in to see how you feel. This is the experience of forgiveness.

WHERE EGO DIVIDES, LOVE CONNECTS.

There is a promise made by the Chassidic masters. Namely, that the practice of Hishtavus is the end of the ego. Yes. This is the promise. This is not attainable overnight. It is an ongoing practice. Amateurs practice until they get it right. Professionals practice until they can't get it wrong. It's time to become a professional at living a joyful and fulfilling life.

CHAPTER FIVE

Living Sameness

I understand. What can I do right now to help me live with sameness?

It is so valuable to be practical. Often we get caught up in the mystique of high ideas. Here are some practical tools for cultivating sameness:

Don't Take Anything Personally: Don Miguel Ruiz, author of Toltec wisdom, used this phrase to describe one of the four major agreements one must make with life in order to live in peace and harmony. The very first thing you can do is make a decision not to be offended anymore. The behavior of others isn't a reason to get stuck in your life. Most of us walk around, conscious or not, looking for ways to be offended. There is always something or someone who is not doing or being what we would like them to be. Remember, the ego is telling you that the world isn't happening the way it should be. Instead of seeing people or situations as frustrating, try viewing them simply as happening. Then realize you are the one judging the situation and turning it into a problem. In his book *The Power of Intention*, Wayne Dyer gave the simple suggestion of shifting your thoughts from what *"they're* doing" to what *"you're* thinking."

For example, when I first started sharing my ideas on social media platforms, I found that there were almost always one or two negative comments about what I chose to say. A colleague of mine reached out to give some love and support, assuring me that all was okay and that I should continue to spread my message. He mentioned that even when hundreds of people positively respond to a post, it's those one or two that get under your skin, and you just can't shake them, so you spend hours of your life in the self-critical mode until you can move past it. I felt the pain of what he must go through when he shares an idea with others that isn't well received. The truth is, however, I didn't feel that way. Of course, I want everyone to appreciate a positive message, but I always focus on the ones that do. It's easy to get offended by a small comment of another person. But why allow them to take up space in your head? In fact, usually people who make hurtful comments are themselves in pain. As the phrase goes, *hurt people, hurt people.*

As a practice, when someone says something you feel is critical, instead of reacting right away, take a breath and smile. On the exhale, in your mind wish them love and healing. You may mentally say *I love you.* Give to others what you want to receive, and in enough time you may find that those exact people become less and less critical because they are being received with less judgement and frustration.

Let Go of Being Right: Another thing you can immediately put into practice is to let go of your need to be right or win. Your soul doesn't see winners and losers. It sees a world where we all grow together. There are no losers in a world where we all come from and return to the same Source. There is no problem in the joy of winning a game or having the right answer. The problem is the attachment to being right. It is the *needing* of it that turns life into a problem; the need to be correct is the source of much conflict.

You can still maintain your opinions, be happy about them, and be peaceful even if someone else disagrees. Imagine a conversation in which someone has a dissenting view and you are able to say, "Wow, what an interesting perspective. I don't see it that way and never thought of it in that light." It doesn't mean that now you do. It just means you have created space for someone else in the conversation. Choose the path of least resistance—which is to say, drop all resistance. It doesn't mean avoid taking action when possible, but rather accepting what is happening and then acting. Practice asking yourself the question: *Would I rather be right or happy? Would I rather win or be at peace?* You can maintain your opinion while being kind, compassionate, and open minded.

As a practice, the next time you engage in what seems to be a debate of right and wrong, watch what happens when you take a relaxing breath and say, "Hmmm . . . I never thought if it that way. I understand where you're coming from. Let me think about it," or "Wow, although it's hard for me to relate, I want to understand you better" and then move forward with the conversation. Watch what happens when you let the conflict go and choose peace instead. Relationships will flourish when you prioritize the loving energy between you above the answer to an argument.

SHIFT YOUR THOUGHTS FROM WHAT "THEY'RE DOING" TO WHAT "YOU'RE THINKING." YOU ARE ONLY ONE THOUGHT AWAY FROM PEACE.

Letting Go of "More": Another path towards letting go is recognizing the mantra of the ego: *more*. The ego is never satisfied. The Talmud says that anyone who receives a hundred wants two hundred. There is the constant need to have more, be more, and appear to be more than what you are right now. Let this idea go altogether. No matter how much you achieve or acquire, your ego will never be satisfied. It will always insist on having more. Don't find yourself in a perpetual state of striving without ever experiencing the taste of arriving. This may be one of the most rewarding aspects of my favorite day of the week: Shabbos. For twenty-five hours a week, sundown Friday evening to nightfall Saturday night, my family and I turn off all of our phones, computers, and any device that accesses the life outside our home, and we are fully focused on what we have and whom we're with. There is no more work, no emails to respond to, no places to go or person to be. It is truly coming to deep communion with the Source. The motto is "all our work is done." It is a full-day meditative experience every week. Try and take a moment now to experience what it would be like if you were finished. Everything you had to *do* was finished, and now you can just *be*. You can let go of the need for more.

As a practice, take an hour and act as if there is truly nothing else to do because you have arrived at your destination. Notice what comes up for you emotionally when you do this. You may notice resistance to the idea that you are finished or anxiety about *what still needs to get done.* Instead of fighting it, witness the emotions and the thoughts as they come up and allow them to pass through you. Sit with them. Hold space for them and acknowledge that they are normal and make sense but that right at this moment, you are *doing* an exercise of *non-doing*, or what is referred to in the Tao as *wu-wei.* Enjoy the peace that comes when you no longer need anything else to be satisfied. You have arrived.

View Compliments and Criticism the Same Way: By nature, the way we do anything is the way we do everything. Although it is worthy to appreciate the love and positive energy that someone sends you in a compliment or praise, once again, the need for a good feeling that praise does for you can, in fact, be a detriment. If, instead of feeling genuine love, the words make you feel special, important, or "better than," then the unfortunate side effect is that criticism will do the same. You will feel inferior, unimportant, and "worse than." It is a constant inner game of comparing and an attempt to add up to some idolized vision of who you think you are supposed to be and who you don't want to be. All of this instead of just being fully who you are.

The next time someone gives you a compliment, see if you can say thank you and appreciate the feelings of love and appreciation they are sending you without holding on to the idea that now you are better because they said it. Say to yourself, "They have been kind for sending me love, and I appreciate our relationship. I am not better now that they think this." A good way to gauge whether or not you are taking the praise the wrong way is by asking yourself how strong the urge is to share this with someone else. You can, of course, do as you wish, but notice the need and inner desire to share and thus get recognition and approval from yet another person outside of yourself.

Take No Credit: In an attempt to feel good about ourselves, we look toward our achievements to determine whether or not we have more or less value. Society seems to demand a certain level of outer accomplishment to allow for the experience of inner wellbeing. Unfortunately, this is only a partial truth and thus a total lie. The side effect is that wherever possible, we look for credit as it bolsters the idea we have in our minds about how valuable, important, and worthy we are. Stop viewing yourself as good or valuable based on your achievements. You have inherent goodness because you are a reflection of God in the world. You are part of perfection. You are a once-in-a-universal-history light. Your achievements may give you temporary satisfaction, but pretty soon you'll be chasing something new. And what if you don't get the recognition you perceive you deserve? More importantly, how much can you really take credit for them anyway? The Zohar, the Mystical Torah Text, says the artist has the desire to paint and then God fills in the inspiration. The builder picks up the bricks, and God builds the building. God is the singer, and you are the song of God.

In the same way, to be inspired means *in spirit,* to have spirit flowing within you. Look at this beautiful passage from the book *A New Earth* by Eckhart Tolle:

> The word enthusiasm comes from the ancient Greek—en and theos, meaning God. And the related word enthousiazein means "to be possessed by God." With enthusiasm you will find that you don't have to do it all by yourself. In fact, there is nothing of significance that you can do by yourself. Sustained enthusiasm brings into existence a wave of creative energy, and all you have to do then is "ride the wave."

Being in a flow state is one of the most pleasurable and creative spaces to experience. Nevertheless, most artists will tell you that they themselves didn't have anything to do with what happened. They were a conduit for something deeper. They express radical humility.

As a practice, try: Take a breath and appreciate what you've done, smiling between you and yourself and feeling grateful, all before you've shared anything with anyone else. Be there fully to witness the miracle that has come through you. You have been the vessel.

Living with this mindset will increase your feeling of gratitude for who you are, what you do, and how your actions get done. You can live in this deep appreciation for all of what life is. No outcomes are yours. All outcomes are good.

NO OUTCOMES ARE YOURS AND ALL OUTCOMES ARE GOOD.

Hishtavus seems to be a nice idea, but everything being the same also sounds somewhat boring and dull. I am not sure I want to live that way.

There is often a concern that if you aren't having highs and lows, your life will be boring. This couldn't be further from the truth. Boring only exists in a world without equanimity. In this state, washing the dishes can be as powerful and potent a moment as prayer. At the heart of it, experiencing this higher state of consciousness allows you to be fully in the presence of something deep, purposeful, and holy, even in the most mundane situations. It is Divine. It is joyous. And it is certainly not boring.

Sameness doesn't mean boring, dull, or numb. No, no, just the opposite. The sameness is beneath the surface. The verse says, "I am God, unchanging." What is the unchanging nature of spirit? Sameness or Oneness is a source of stillness, love, power, pure energy, and joy. It is perfection. It's not an *idea* of love or *perfect* love, but the Truth behind what these words point to. It is the inner knowing, the experience of the truth that is Hishtavus.

Yes . . . to the ego it might seem scary because it means giving up something it has grown accustomed to labeling as good, fun, or better. But this is like telling a drug addict that his life will be better when he stops getting high all the time and him responding, *Yes, but I love getting high so much.* It's like telling someone who struggles with obesity that if she keeps eating high fructose corn syrup, it will affect her heart, and her response is *Yes . . . but I don't want to give up the pleasures of life.*

The goal is not to disengage from the journey, but to fully engage in it from a place of peace, a place of wholeness.

There might appear to be less "action" on the surface, but with equanimity we trade it in for something more concrete, more real, and more alive. How many times have we caught ourselves doing something because we are restless and couldn't find peace right where we were? When we're looking to escape the present moment, to escape what's happening, including our boredom, we make decisions based on what type of high it will give us. But just as to every action there is an equal and opposite reaction, for every high we crave, there is an equal and opposite low. Only in a world at peace can we cease to descend. And it's exactly in this peace that we will find meaningful joy and positivity, light and creativity. The most innovative ideas on the planet were born out of this state. David Burkus of Harvard Business Review explains that *"taking a break from the problem and focusing on something else entirely gives the mind some time to release its fixation on the same solutions and let the old pathways fade from memory. Then, when you return to the original problem, your mind is more open to new possibilities— eureka moments."* Creativity doesn't emerge from the running, it happens in the rest. It happens when you are in flow. Yes, you will continue running, doing, and achieving. Yes, you will continue to live with high positive energy, but it isn't stemming from a need or impulse to fill a void but rather the innate nature of life to create, expand, and love. This is a totally different type of living—one that most people only taste in sporadic moments of joy when they are totally present and in the flow.

Some people mistake sameness as indifference, coldness, hesitation, or withdrawal, but this is incorrect; these are forms of aversion—lack of acceptance. In truth, sameness is a practice of accepting the world as it is and connecting anyway. The still mind accepts the fact of pain in our world. It understands suffering and cruelty as part of the world, which is dominated by ignorance. In stillness, we engage and respond with intention regardless of the challenge.

Read this beautiful passage from Judith Orloff's *Emotional Freedom* that captures the idea so succinctly:

"Emotional freedom doesn't mean becoming bland, numbing our feelings, or spewing them indiscriminately towards others. It entails striving to develop everything that is positive within us as well as being accountable for our full spectrum of feelings, mastering them, and realizing we're so much larger than they are."

What about emotions? Aren't we supposed to feel great, and also sad? Aren't emotions a good thing?

Emotions are a wonderful and important part of our human experience. Through our emotions we gain access to our energy, and all of our feelings flow through our emotional epicenter: the heart. Is there sadness in loss? Yes, of course. Is their joy in birth? Yes, of course. Does it feel really good to be in a happy mood? Is it depressing to be depressed? The answer to all of these questions is obvious. So, indeed, there is great room for feelings and emotions because they are the colors of life. They are the energy we experience and the vibrations we send out into the world around us. They impact how we perform, how we behave, and on a spiritual level, even what we draw to us.

And yet, there can be feelings on the surface and deep peace underneath the surface. Imagine the waves crashing one upon another out in the ocean. On the surface there is constant movement and change. No two moments are the same. But underneath the clamoring of the ocean surface there exists a deep stillness of the unified water below. So is the ocean in constant movement or deep stillness? Both. Equanimity and the peace of sameness can be experienced at the depth of your consciousness while you are aware of different emotions that appear on the surface. The difference is that you do not identify so much with the emotion that it takes over and hijacks your perception. You remain who you are, in the seat of your consciousness, aware of the stirrings.

You can feel the feelings and yet still have the ability to choose and act instead of reacting to life unconsciously. A person can feel sadness and gratitude at the same time—sadness over the loss of someone and gratitude for the presence he/she had in their life. Surface-level happiness is generated by our interpretation. There is a deeper joy that comes with feelings of peace and love, which are innate feelings existing beyond circumstance. By this I mean they are your natural state. Underneath the baggage we carry, we are all happy people. The soul knows no other experience. Your soul is singing in every moment. The fact that we don't experience our innate happiness consciously is because of the wall blocking us—the wall between who we are and who we *think* we are. It has been said that there is no *way* to happiness. Happiness *is* the way. You will be happy when you strip away everything that is not of your true nature.

THERE IS NO WAY TO HAPPINESS. HAPPINESS IS THE WAY.

Furthermore, emotions are a measuring stick by which we can measure how we are interpreting reality. When you interpret reality as good, you feel happy. When you interpret reality as negative, you feel sad or angry. But this is only a reflection of how you view and experience the world. Therefore, seeing clearly is of prime importance. How you *feel* informs you of what you *believe* right now. The more we integrate this clear perspective into our lives, the more our emotional barometer will reflect our inner state with consistent feelings of joy, peace, and harmony.

Emotions are not a problem. Craving or aversion, which are both forms of attachment, are what create extended pain, or what we call suffering. Attachment comes when we can't let go of something that happened in the past or we decide we won't be happy until something changes according to our expectations for the future. If we crave the continuation or intensification of a joyful experience, then when it inevitably changes, we will experience dissatisfaction in direct proportion to the strength of our craving. Thus, all negative emotions are not defined by what happens to you but by your inner response to what happens. Emotions are real, but they are not reality. They are merely the reality you still choose to see in any given moment.

But what about the fact that life does get hard and some problems are really difficult to manage?

We are generally under the assumption that life *should* be easy. But again, whenever there is a "should" in our mind, it's because we have decided what life should be instead of paying attention to what life is. I suffered from this disease called *should.* It used to haunt me. I'd often feel that situations should be different, people shouldn't have done what they did, and I should already be somewhere else and achieving something else. The word "should" belongs to the ego. One of its main tactics is to convince you that things *should* be different. The reality is that things *are* as they are and do not need to be different. How do I know? Because that is how they are.

Instead of fighting the challenge with resistance, feel into the pain and hold compassionate space for your feelings. When you start to feel, you start to heal. Feeling into the pain of a difficult situation is being fully present with your experience instead of wishing it were different. In this acceptance you may find yourself relieved somewhat and are now more able to choose your next course of action.

CHAPTER SIX

Do Problems Really Exist?

So does this mean I should accept everything I don't like because that's just how it is? This sounds like I need to be totally complacent and not address my problems.

Challenges can either awaken you or pull you into a deeper sleep.

I believe it begins with clarifying the language we use. Our general assumption is that all challenges are "bad," and in this light we call them "problems." But are there really problems? What if we changed the way we looked at our difficulties? The

Latin root of the word "problem" is *problema*, which means *throwing forth a question or situation*. Situations arise, and they can be viewed as a question. The question goes like this: *What are you going to do about . . . ?* It's a question about what you are going to do. How you are going to respond. The question is not *how do you feel about this?*

We often walk around assuming the basic question is *how do I feel about this?* And very often the answer we give is *I really don't like this.* When we assume this question, we are bound to go for a bumpy ride. Our inner answer to any question about our feelings sounds something like *good, bad, good, great, amazing, terrible, bad, worse, better, good,* and so on. We set ourselves up to judge and assess everything that happens because there is another underlying question behind *how do you feel*; namely, *is this good or bad?*

What happens when we drop this question and move deeply into a totally new experience? What happens when you see life as being part of something much more vast, grand, and infinitely loving? What happens if the underlying assumption changes to *"All things are good; there are no mistakes in the universe, and I am being taken care of and guided in all situations"*? What if, for a moment, we choose to see life through a different lens?

We can choose to see our life situation as an enemy, an obstacle, or a means to an end in any situation; this means we're defending, hating, defeating, overcoming, and using life. Or, we can choose to see life (and particularly our "problems") as a friend to love, a detour to embrace, and an opportunity to appreciate and experience.

The Universe is always saying, *I will be whatever you want me to be. I'll treat you how you treat me.* If you see circumstance as a problem, it will be a problem for you, won't it? If you choose to see opportunities, what type of action do you think you'll make in response? We respond with better quality when we see things with a higher-quality perspective. Don't create any more pain for yourself by resisting what is and by wanting to be someone else, somewhere else, or doing something else. We only have two options: accept the unacceptable when there is nothing to do about it, or take action. Sometimes taking action is self-defense. Sometimes it is saying something, and sometimes it means to leave a particular situation. If there is nothing you can *do* about something, then to maintain an "inner no" to life is somewhat of insanity. It would serve you better to have an "inner yes" to life, accept, and move forward.

THE UNIVERSE WILL ALWAYS TREAT YOU THE WAY YOU TREAT IT.

THIS IS THE RULE OF MEASURE FOR MEASURE.

Every challenge contains within it a hidden light we just can't see yet. They say we need to learn how to roll with the punches. When approaching this topic, I think of this acronym *R.O.L.L with the punches*. See all the *punches* as:

- **R**eminders—of what's important and what's real.

- **O**pportunities—that have not been revealed yet.

- **L**essons—to be learned.

- **L**eading—in a new and significant direction you might never have taken otherwise.

Remember that anything we label as "bad" is really just a portal, a channel, and a reminder of our destiny. Use it. Use the hard experiences as opportunities to go deeper into your true nature, which is the light you truly are. The love that you are. The creative person that you are. The kind person that you are.

The forgiving person that you are. The powerful person that you are. The soulful person that you are. Let go of whatever is false and grab onto truth.

A practice that is incredibly useful is to keep a *reminder journal.* Mentally scroll through your life and identify the times where it was clear to you that what on the surface appeared as trouble was in fact a reminder, opportunity, lesson, or led you in a new direction toward something important. Keeping track of these experiences strengthens your resolve and consciousness of living with a higher order. You may borrow stories and lessons from others that have inspired you as well. There is no limit to where you can draw inspiration from on your journey toward awakening.

CHAPTER SEVEN

Awareness Is The Key

All right. I'm with you. It sounds easier said than done, but better done than only said. Help me understand what you're talking about. What must I do or stop doing to experience more Hishtavus?

One practice. Many portals. Influential teacher Ajahn Chah would say that "if you let go a little, you will have a little peace. If you let go a lot, you will have a lot of peace. If you let go completely, you will know complete peace and freedom." But you cannot let go until you know what you are letting go of. The only real way to find yourself is to discover what you are not.

When you let go of what you are not, all that's left will be your true self.

It all begins with awareness. It all begins with seeing. The seeing is freeing. What I mean is that until you begin to pick up on the subtle and yet deeply entrenched belief system you're living with, it will be very hard to change anything. But this is not just about change. It's more about letting go of your mask. The mask is a belief you decided to agree with, and it has become the lens through which you see the world. It shapes the entire paradigm of your life. Seen in this light, a belief is an agreement we have each made with reality. Through conditioning we've signed a contract between us and ourselves about how we perceive the universe.

Where did this belief system come from? Every belief is really just a thought, but one you've had so many times that it has become your automatic-response thinking. It happens so fast, you are not even always aware that you are living this way. Thus you take it to be true without question, and it remains subconscious. It then becomes very hard to discern if you're not looking for it. Because of this, it is easier to start by noticing your speech patterns. The tongue is the quill of the heart, and you can trace what you say back to your thoughts. You can become a witness and begin to notice when you are not experiencing Hishtavus.

THE SEEING IS FREEING.
BECOME THE WITNESS OF YOUR MIND.

Catch yourself using the language of the ego. Remember, beneath the surface, your soul sees the sameness, the Oneness, and the innate good in all people, places, and things. It is aware of the Divine purpose in all that is and the Infinite Intelligence guiding and directing life. The ego, however, speaks in a language that reflects disbelief in this loving presence. It speaks in a way that separates, compares, and judges. Let's take a deeper look into some of the ways we can discern between the two voices.

COMPARING

Be on the lookout for comparing. When we compare ourselves to others, we are looking at the surface level of reality and making a judgment based on what we see with our eyes and nothing more. All it takes is turning on your social media, and immediately it's compare, compare, and compare. You walk down the street and see a couple who looks happier than you do, and again you're back to comparing. Comparing is a facet of fear. Fear that you are not good enough or that life isn't good enough. It always comes back to this. To be clear, I am not discussing comparing the difference in the quality of the different types of tiles you might be planning to use for your kitchen, nor am I discussing comparing who is more qualified to fill a position at work or who is more compatible to date. These are examples of comparing at the surface level for a surface reason. Obviously, you do need good tiles, competent employees, and a partner you can get along with.

The comparing I am talking about is when you label one person better or worse, good or bad, fat or thin, pretty or ugly, smart or dumb, in the context of what you believe about their essence. Yes, if your child is too small to ride on the rollercoaster, you better make that judgment for the sake of the child. But the mistake is to then use that judgment of being small to imply a general weakness or smallness of essence.

King David said, "I am a worm." What did he mean by this? The intention of his statement is that you should not compare yourself to others because at the deepest level of truth, there is no difference between you and a worm. Both serve God and the highest order, but in different ways. See yourself as equal and the same to all life. See all of life as equal and the same as you.

Instead of comparing, see if you can just let those thoughts go. In the beginning it can be difficult because we are so habituated to comparing. Ask yourself this question: *How does making comparisons help?*

GOSSIP

Making comparisons often expresses itself in gossip, which is one of the worst forms of ego. We gossip in order to strengthen our sense of self, which is none other than the ego. Putting others down gives you a momentary feeling of knowing more, being better, and having some authority. Sage wisdom has described gossip as an action that pushes away God's presence and spiritual experience. Begin to notice how you feel when a conversation filled with gossip is over. Yes, in the moment it might have felt pleasurable, but when it's over, you are likely to notice a subtle sense of discomfort, and this is the feeling that lingers. The same is true for any ego-invested pleasure. It feels good in the moment, and then it's followed by a feeling of pain. It's the gossip hangover.

Make it your practice to notice gossip when it starts and remember that it is going to take away your sense of true Self. It is going to strengthen something that will ultimately cause you more pain. Is it really worth it? Yes, you want to speak about how upset you are when your best friend ditches you for somebody else, and you have all the verbal ammunition ready, but remember that you are not just hurting others, you are hurting yourself when you bad-mouth another human being. Is it really worth it? This goes for listening to gossip too. When we sit and take in someone else's judgments, it becomes harder for us to see objectively, and our minds get clouded. If you truly want to be happy, the poison of gossip has to stop.

OPINIONS

Anytime you state your opinion when it isn't being asked for, or your opinion is not productive, is likely to be an expression of ego trying to show it exists: *You see, I also have thought about this and know something. I also have ideas about this.* Here is a practice you can put to the test today: The next time someone offers you an opinion about something, just listen. See if you can do it without giving your own opinion. Just hear what they have to say without adding your two cents. You might find this harder than you think. With enough practice, you may find that *not* giving your opinion gives you more satisfaction than telling everyone how you feel about things. The peace you will experience is true contentment.

COMPLAINING

Then there is complaining, the mother of all negativity. Every complaint is a negative judgment about something or someone else. There is no greater resistance. What benefit is there in complaining? All it does is make other people aware that you are unhappy. So why do we complain? We complain because we believe if we express why we are upset, our resentments will be justified. But there are no justified resentments. There is a saying that goes, "Fight for your limitations, and they are yours." You can justify all the resentments you have, but in the end you are left resisting and resentful, which is not what you desire. I don't mean there are no good reasons to be upset. I mean there are no good reasons to hold on and create a drama about something that will just take up space in your mind and body for longer than is needed.

EVERY COMPLAINT IS A JUDGMENT THAT WILL QUICKLY TURN INTO PAIN.

The Proverb says: "The complainer separates from God." The implication of every complaint is *this should not be happening, I don't want to be here, I don't want to do this, I am being treated unfairly*, etc. These are thoughts of "should and shouldn't." They are the prime factor in all unhappy moments. They turn the present moment into an enemy. Complaining, speaking negatively about people or situations, and labeling are all ego strategies to protect itself. We tell ourselves, *the world is wrong; I am right*. Every complaint is a little story your mind has made up that you completely believe.

Complaints come in many forms; whether you complain aloud or in thought makes no difference. We even complain when we are held back from doing things we think are positive. It happens quite often that we intend to do something we see as good, loving, positive, or spiritual and then "things go the wrong way." Something happens, a phone call, a mistake, a traffic jam.

You name it. And now, not only are you not able to perform the good you intended, you are frustrated and feeling like you've wasted your time.

Know that even if your intention was to study, pray, or work on your spiritual practice—including performing acts of love and kindness—if you are withheld, all is still well and good. Don't let it upset you. Instead, see that this has become your immediate spiritual practice. Your assignment in the moment is to surrender, accept, and keep an eye open for the higher good. There is love encased in all frustrations. Your challenge is your opportunity. Until now you might have been judging your life situations as good or bad, spiritual or profane, but you can stop and bring awareness to the fact that the place upon which you stand is holy ground. There are no accidents.

You might be thinking, *But what am I supposed to do when I get upset?* Another Proverb says: "Patience quiets struggle." Non-reaction and acceptance of one's situation quiets one's internal struggle. Similarly, non-reaction to the ego in others is one of the most effective ways of not only going beyond one's own ego but also of helping others go beyond their egos. The good in you brings out the good in others. The presence in you can bring out the presence in others. The next time you feel like complaining, see what happens if you can catch yourself before you start, and just let it pass through you. No, I don't mean let the ideas sit in your mind and bubble over. I mean let go and accept whatever has happened and move forward into the next moment, fully present with whatever your attention needs to be on now. You might just change the world.

Have you ever had an experience that caused you to be upset about something or at someone and then boom—something really significant happens that causes you to totally forget what you were worried about? The power goes out. A fender bender on the road. Someone you know has gotten sick or, better yet, has been given a great honor. By the time you get back to reality after hearing this other news, what you were focused on before doesn't seem so significant anymore. It seems silly to fight or complain over a little spilled coffee. These are the moments when our attention is moved to another point so rapidly and deeply that we have become present somewhere else. When we are living in the present, energy that is trapped in the past is pulled into the present and made available to us, never to return again unless we mistakenly obsess over it anew.

In the book *A New Earth*, Eckhart Tolle tells the story of spiritual teacher J. Krishnamurti, who toured the world for nearly fifty years, talking about spirituality. One day toward the end of his life, he said to the audience, "Would you like to know my secret? I don't mind what happens."

I don't mind means I don't put my ego, my mind, into what happens. My opinion of it doesn't matter. The surface layer is a relative truth and not the definition of my reality. *I don't mind* means *I don't judge*. I know there is more that doesn't have to do with my opinion. It's all the same to me.

"I DON'T MIND WHAT HAPPENS."

ALLOWING AND LOVING

"In all of your ways, know Him." —Proverbs. This is the practice of not minding, of totally letting go of outcomes, dropping expectations, and detaching your opinion from reality. In Torah language this is called *Bitachon*: trust or certainty. To live with trust is to live alive while learning to trust the Universe, to trust God, to trust there is an infinite love guiding and directing all things. This is the foundation of equanimity. This is Hishtavus.

The Talmud says there are three types of people who shine like the sun. They exude light and radiate the kind of energy we all want more of in our lives. These are people who (1) do not return one insult for another, (2) act from love, and (3) can accept challenges with joy. What do these three have in common? They have all let go of their ego. They live with sameness. They are not moved or disturbed by some surface-level phenomenon; they have a spiritual mindset. They are at a level of consciousness that is aware of the game, aware of the dream, but not attached to it. They don't take the thoughts and judgments of others personally, and thus they are at peace and shine the light within them out to the world.

To act from love means to live because it resonates with your very being, not because it pacifies someone else's expectations of what you are supposed to do or who you are supposed to be. To accept challenges with love is to know that deep within all of creation there is only love, and whatever unfolds is of a higher order of good, visible or not. You are welcome to try the powerful technique of not immediately responding to insult and criticism. Say nothing, not even something good, for through the positive opinion, your ego will awaken and drag you into negativity. Stay in silence. Only after the feeling of needing to defend yourself has passed can you respond from a place of clarity with a still mind. This is a powerful spiritual practice. It means consciously choosing to allow your ego to be diminished without needing to immediately restore it.

CHOOSE TO RADIATE YOUR POWERFUL ENERGY.

Experiment with this every now and then. After the initial shock of being hurt, you might sense an inner spaciousness that feels very alive. You haven't been diminished at all. In fact, you have expanded. Instead of becoming less, you have become more, and the true power of who you are will shine the way it was meant to.

As you grow in non-reaction externally, make it your practice to monitor your inner dialogue. Your thoughts are the subtle level of reaction that runs deeper than your speech. Though it requires more attention and awareness, this is where the practice should take you. This will lead you to the peace you seek.

But what about when it isn't someone else who put you down? What about when you are frustrated or even hate yourself for not living up to your own expectations?

The most insidious way the ego expresses itself is through self-destruction and sabotage. All of the pathways to awareness mentioned above can and should be used to learn how you treat yourself. Self-compassion is the way forward. There is a great story I love that points to the truth of this idea:

A student asked his teacher, "Why is everyone happy except me?" The teacher responded by saying, "Because they have learned to see goodness and beauty everywhere." Puzzled, the student asked again, "But why don't I see goodness and beauty everywhere?" The teacher smiled, pointed to the student's heart, and said, "Because you cannot see outside of yourself what you fail to see inside of yourself."

If you pay attention, you will begin to notice how we compare ourselves to others or to some phantom self we think we are meant to stack up to. We gossip about ourselves to ourselves, we call ourselves names that are insulting and degrading, and we really give ourselves grief. We complain about how we're failures and we get things wrong, and we seem to have an opinion about everything that has to do with us.

Let it all go.

See these thoughts for what they are: thoughts—no more and no less. They are as unreal as other people's opinions of you. Only when you let go of the negative thoughts that take up your mental space can the light of joy, peace, and positivity fill the void. There is no peace in a mind that is an enemy to itself.

YOU CANNOT SEE OUTSIDE OF YOURSELF

WHAT YOU FAIL TO SEE INSIDE OF YOURSELF.

I get what you're saying: awareness is the key. But is there anything I can do that isn't just about paying attention to my thoughts or noticing my speech?

Yes. Here are a number of practices, each deserving of their own chapter or even a book. I will mention them to you in brevity with the knowing that as they resonate with you, you will dive deeper into them.

JOURNALING

Keep a consciousness journal. Include accounts of the people, places, and scenarios that trigger unrest within you. Just writing these things down can help process your painful experiences and cultivate an awareness of what brings your personal negativity to the surface. Don't make a big deal out of what type of journal you use, how big, what type of paper, or if it's on a device. Just begin. In his book *Stillness is the Key,* Ryan Holiday refers to journaling as "spiritual windshield wipers." It couldn't be more true. This is a truly rewarding practice.

Journaling need not take more than a few minutes. Sit quietly with yourself and scan your previous day. In the beginning, don't look for anything subtle. Start by writing down a couple events that stand out clearly in your mind. Then, write down how you felt and how you responded—if your response was significant. A couple examples: *She forgot to return my call—I was angry—I wrote her a nasty email,* or *I burnt the dinner—I was really down on myself—I went to drown my self-loathing in YouTube videos.*

Over time, you will notice there are certain people, discussions, opinions, and even places you go that awaken deep-seated pain and resentment. For some, this might be when people comment on their appearance. For others, it strikes when their intelligence is questioned. The ego is triggered by anything that threatens its existence. Try this practice for a few weeks and see how much more conscious you become throughout the day. The more awareness you create, the more power to choose you'll have the next time a similar scenario shows up. Keeping a journal will help increase your awareness.

MEDITATION

In addition to writing in your journal, there is no substitute for the quiet of meditation. Something happens within when we let go of the noise of the outer world, as well as the incessant chatter of the mind. This is an opportunity to experience that which your five senses don't detect. Spending time daily to relax your mind and sit in silence is a gift you can give yourself and everyone around you. You meet yourself in that peaceful place.

Sit in the stillness. Sit in the quiet. Make it your spiritual practice to do nothing at all. It has been said that if prayer is speaking to the Divine, meditation is listening to what It has to say. Learn to listen in the quiet and carry the stillness with you everywhere you go. This will allow you to maintain conscious contact with your Source.

In this quiet space, you free yourself from the incessant thinking of the mind. You touch the place of true liberation. You can take the first step right now by taking a few moments to listen to the voice inside your head. Pay attention to the thoughts you are thinking and just watch. Be the witnessing presence. Don't judge the thoughts as good or bad, just see them and note them for what they are. If you judge them, know that it is the same voice coming in through another door. The practice of watching your inner world is just as or more important than being aware of your surroundings.

Creativity emerges in the space of non-doing and paves the way for newly inspired action. Make the time for meditation, and you will be grateful for the rest of your life.

PRAYER

We often underestimate the power and elevation that prayer offers. It doesn't matter what your relationship is with the Divine Intelligence that guides our reality. All that is needed is authentic engagement. It's better to have a heart without the right words than to have words without a right heart. Prayer is an offering, a letting go, and a stepping aside.

IT'S BETTER TO HAVE A HEART WITHOUT THE RIGHT WORDS
THAN TO HAVE WORDS WITHOUT A RIGHT HEART.

When we pray, we get out of the way. The most powerful force of the ego is the desire to control outcomes and situations, people and their views, and anything and everything that can be dreamed up by our ego. But the truth is we are not in control of anything other than how we see the unfolding of our lives. The controlling energy of the ego comes between all good things and us. It ruins relationships, strips the joy away from the process, and undoes the playful curiosity of our inner child. We carry a load with us everywhere we go.

This baggage is the feeling that we need to control everything that happens in our life. But we need to let it go and give it back to God, give it back to the power of love. Remember: no outcomes are yours, and all outcomes are good. Yes, indeed, we must put forth the effort to accomplish everything we wish to experience, but then we must let go and yield to the higher order and knowing of God. The book *A Course in Miracles* says, "for the memory of God can dawn only in a mind that chooses to remember and that has relinquished the insane desire to control reality." Prayer is the doorway that allows us to turn over our desires to a Higher Source that is all-knowing, all-powerful, and all-loving. Many people have been conditioned to relate to a warped vision of God. It's for that reason that I often refer to God or God's Presence as Love, Truth, Being, The Universe, and other words that are less threatening.

The letters G, O, and D themselves do not have intrinsic meaning. They are a metaphor or symbol pointing you in the direction of the meaning for which it stands. The power of this Presence is beyond name and form. It is loving, compassionate, and intentional. There is guidance, direction, and assistance. And it is personal. The more we connect with the idea of a loving Higher Power, the more we see that It is directing life in the most perfect way, and the more we are able to pray and surrender to that Power, the more we are able to feel peace in our own lives.

WHEN YOU PRAY, YOU GET OUT OF THE WAY.

PRESENCE

"And now, what is it that God asks of you?" — Deuteronomy. We all question what we are doing here. What is meant to be the focus of our being in this world? The verse begins, "And now." Now is what is asked of you. To be fully present. Fully in the now. To let go of the past and also the future. To be fully here where you are in the present moment. Because if you can't be here and now, then you can't be there and then. For when the there and then become the here and now, you will be there and then again. You will only ever be able to enjoy the future if you learn to enjoy the now. This is the meaning of the sage line, *"If not now, when?"* There is only ever this moment.

How much time is spent dwelling on the past or worrying about the future? Yes, the past is important because it holds a lesson for the present, and the future is important because it holds the dream of our destiny. But after we've learned from our past and created our dream, it's time to come back home. The only moment that matters, as far as you are concerned, is the moment you are in right now. A great sage was asked, "What page of the Talmud is the best one?" And he responded, "The one I am learning now."

No matter what you are doing, where you are, and whomever you are with, strive to be there fully. Yes, you might notice something inside of you dragging your attention to another person, place, thing, or time, but leave it be. Let that thought pass through you, and be where you are. Wherever you are is exactly where you are supposed to be right now. How do I know? Because that is where you are.

The Hebrew word for God, referenced to as *Havaya*, means "The Eternal Present." The more you live in the present, the more you are one with God.

ONE THOUSAND TOMORROWS WILL NEVER BE AS GOOD AS ONE TODAY.

GRATITUDE

If you are looking for a daily practice to help you experience equanimity, there is nothing more powerful than the holy space of gratitude. First thing in the morning, take time to appreciate the precious gift of life that is yours, everything you have, and all of your relationships. Just a few minutes of sincere gratitude can totally shift the nature of your day. Gratitude is an elixir. Where the ego sees disdain, the soul sees a gift.

To live with deep appreciation for life is to be truly present. To recognize good is to truly live with the Divine and walk with God. Gratitude is the foundation for all of the blessings in the world and for a calm inner space. With gratitude, we remind ourselves of all the good that has already transpired, the good that is now, and the good that is going to be. An ancient practice is to make the first few words you say every morning *I am grateful.* This simple act, when done with the whole of your being, can radically change your life.

FEEL FEELINGS

Feel whatever you are feeling. This doesn't mean you are obligated to scream at the person you are upset with. Sit quietly and feel your feelings deeply. They are happening now, in the moment. Be with them. Learn from them. Have compassion for them. Feelings are real, but they are not reality. They are a reflection of how we view events and the people around us.

ACT THE PART

Here is something you can do to aid in your transformation: Act as if you are already who you want to be. This means to throw yourself fully into it. Feel the feelings of joy and love in your face and your tone of voice, sit or stand up straight, and walk with the confidence you would if you were really feeling this way. Even if you feel like defending yourself from an insult, act as if you really don't mind at all. Remember, we are so habituated in the other direction that it's not going to feel natural in the beginning. Act as if you are already the person you want to be. Assume the feelings you wish to experience.

ACT AS IF YOU ARE ALREADY THE PERSON YOU WANT TO BE.

ACT AS IF YOU ARE ALREADY FEELING WHAT YOU WANT TO FEEL.

CHAPTER EIGHT

All Is Of The Highest Good

I want to believe everything that you're saying. I feel like somewhere in my heart of hearts, I already know what you mean. But how do I consciously unlock this inner knowing and experience it more in my day-to-day life?

This knowing stands at the heart of this book. Knowing is everything. In fact, the Talmud says: "If knowing you have acquired, what are you lacking? If knowing you are lacking, what have you acquired? True poverty is only that of knowing." So what is this knowing? The truth is, it's not something that can be fully expressed in words. We try the best we can, but in the end, it's so personal to the self that only you know its true meaning. Nevertheless, qualities of this inner experience include:

1. Awareness and sense of a Universal Intelligence guiding and directing the events in your life with purposeful intention.

2. Awareness and sense of your essence being something not of this world, despite being in the world.

3. Awareness and sensing the good and love that is embedded in the fabric of creation.

Knowing is the way in to God. Knowing is living with the clear notion that there is an all-powerful, loving, and personal God, a Creator Who is guiding, directing, and moving the world toward the highest good. Knowing is recognizing there is no chaos and nothing is random; there are no coincidences and no accidents. Your birthplace, your parents, your skills or lack thereof are all designed to help you achieve your unique purpose.

Meditate on this:

Everything emanates from the same Source. Life is unfolding from the One being that is Truth. There is a prayer that says: "Blessed is the One that spoke the world into being." This is a reminder of Who is telling the story of life. When we go deeply into this, we remember the story is a good story. The story is a Godly story. There is a Divine need for everything that happens. Everything and everyone matters on a cosmic level because all that exists are cosmic matters of a Divine intelligence, of a higher order of thinking and seeing reality. The cosmos is not chaotic; actually, the word "cosmos" means order. A Divine order.

THERE ARE NO COINCIDENCES. NOTHING IS RANDOM.

Jacob Joseph of Polonne, known as the Toldos Yaakov Yosef, wrote the first Chassidic work ever published. As one of the Baal Shem Tov's prime disciples, he would say: "I practice Hishtavus by seeing everything as being from God, and so it is of the highest good, the deepest love, and most sincere compassion. I put love, joy, and the infinitude of God in my mind whenever anything happens that seemingly stands against me." Know that things are, in fact, working out. Things are going your way. Things are perfect and will only ever get better. Even when we descend, it is only for a higher ascent afterwards. We fall to rise. We bend our knees to jump even higher.

That which is real is that which never changes. That which never changes is the still and complete love within all of creation. When you lose your sense of connection to this stillness, you lose touch with who you are. When you lose touch with who you are, you start to get lost in the world. There are no accidents. There are no mistakes in the universe. Know this. God wants more for you than you could ever want for yourself.

Knowing is recognizing the truth of who you are. You are a spiritual being who is learning, developing, and growing in a physical reality. You and all of your actions are perfect, even when they seem imperfect. It is the deepest acceptance and love of self and life. Every breath you take, everything you say, the mere fact of your being, brings joy to creation and the Creator and enhances the presence of love in the world. Even when you have seemingly made mistakes, your presence is Divine and part of something greater. In this moment, you get a new opportunity to connect with the ineffable. Right now, you can undo past mistakes with a fresh desire and aligned intention to grow and develop. Instead of living with guilt and shame over the past, you can choose a new perspective and learn from it. Life can be win or learn, not win or lose. In this context, even your failures are opportunities and provide more growth and experiences of love and good in the world. Every moment, no matter how trivial it might seem, is important to the grand picture and your part in it. Your engagement in the world is holy, and every moment holds the prospect of spiritual connection and joy.

LIFE ISN'T WIN OR LOSE.
IT IS WIN OR LEARN.

This knowing is the knowing of Oneness. Of unity and knowing that there is nothing separate from you in this world. You are connected to all that is, all that ever was, and all that will be. Separateness is the tool of the ego. You are a soul, a spark of the Infinite, shining for a brief time in this physical reality. There is so much more to who you are. The majority of your being is invisible and undetectable. Much of your being is not even in your body. We have come to rely so heavily on our senses that it has become hard to trust our inner knowing.

When you let go of the ego, your life starts to slow down. You're not in such a rush because you know that all things will happen exactly when and how they are supposed to. You do not have to prove yourself to anyone because you are working in harmony with the greatest Partner imaginable. Life is a partnership and a co-creation.

It is an inner knowing that the world is filled with abundance. There is no lack other than in the mind. There is blessing everywhere. So often we are convinced that we are in the wrong place and the wrong time, or we believe we don't have enough. There is no such thing as the wrong place or the wrong time. This is the illusion: we think we know better than whatever the infinite-loving direction could have possibly designed.

Everything happens at the right time. Answers to questions are delivered when they are supposed to be. Questions remain where they are meant to remain. We find our partners in life not a moment before we are supposed to find them, and when we don't, it's because there are other plans. The reason we experience pain is because our plans don't always align with our Divine purpose.

ON THE DIVINE CLOCK,
EVERYTHING HAPPENS AT EXACTLY THE RIGHT TIME.

It is knowing clarity and banishing doubt from all thinking. It is only the persuasive power of doubt that causes us to fall into negativity. When we are connected to Truth, we are joyous and flower with new creativity. Doubt is the enemy of growth. Doubt holds us back from movement. It is better to try and fail than fail to try. Your life is good today. Your life is good now.

Here are several ways to plug back into your sacred space:

Faith is a gateway. It is a portal into this knowing. Faith is about aligning your mind with what you already know deep in your heart. It has less to do with an idea in your mind and more to do with how right-minded thinking unlocks the treasure chest you've been sitting on your whole life.

Meditation is another. Spending time in silence allows for the sediments of your mind to drop to the bottom of the mental barrel. In this lucid space, you can see more clearly and draw insight into your present moments. It doesn't take very long. Just a few minutes in deep silence can recalibrate your entire inner system.

The words you speak contain the energy of your presence. As I've mentioned, the tongue is the quill of the heart. This connection works in both directions. You may also choose to direct your heart with the words you choose to say. As a practice, when you choose to speak words of consciousness, faith, and love, you are redirecting your focus and attention back onto the truth you seek to experience. Intentionally choosing to use words of kindness, love, and joy will bring you back to this place of peace and knowing.

There is no substitute for applying what you already know to be true. Something to ponder: Are there practices you know already work for you? Where can you integrate them in your life even more? Study ever so closely the journal of your heart.

But I thought Hishtavus was about rising above good and bad . . . I guess I have to ask, What do you mean when you say all is good?

This question is maybe the most important question one can ever ask. In life as we know it, we normally associate what is good with what is desirable, and what is bad with what is undesirable. We associate what we desire with pleasure and gain, and we associate what we don't desire with pain or loss.

However, this is only a relative good and a relative bad. When I say "all is good," I mean absolute good that is beyond measure, beyond time, and beyond our own opinions.

Absolute good can be defined as that which is desirable to God, not to the individual. This good is the opinion of a higher truth. It's a revelation and a light. It's when intention shines through. Good is related to growth, learning, and purpose. Good is Godly. It is the evolution of human consciousness. Yes, if we could see the whole picture it would also be desirable to us. Nevertheless, our perspective is limited.

So when is life good? Always. Because every moment includes the desirable unfolding of God's plan. Thus, good is really perfection. Even when the world is imperfect, it is perfectly imperfect. When we see the world in this way, our reality becomes based on the underlying truth that all is One and all is Holy. Our ability to experience this truth is the most pleasurable and desirable experience—the highest "good." Our inability to experience this truth is what gives rise to the pain and other undesirable feelings that we label as "bad." We see things as broken because our ability to perceive God in them is broken. We see things as missing when our ability to see God in them is missing. We get caught in the illusion, and we feel the pain of being seemingly separate. This is why King David said, "It is the closeness to God that I define as good."

The Talmud says everything that happens is for the highest good. "This, too, is for the good," Nachum Ish Gamzu would say. What "too"? Even the things that don't appear that way. There is a well-known story about Rabbi Akiva, a disciple of Nachum, who was traveling with a donkey, a candle, and a rooster. One evening he entered a city, hoping to find shelter, and was turned away. "Everything God does is for the good," he said and spent the night in a nearby field outside the city. His lamp blew out in the wind. "Everything God does is for the good," he said again. His rooster was then mangled by a fox. "Everything God does is for the good," he repeated. Finally, his donkey was devoured by a lion. Once again, Rabbi Akiva repeated his mantra, "Everything God does is for the good."

In the morning, he ventured into the city and realized that bandits had attacked during the night, capturing many people. Had he found a place to stay, he too might have been captured. Had the bandits noticed a lamp in the field or heard his animals, he also might have been spotted. Instead, his life was saved by all of the seemingly "bad" things that happened to him.

We might not see, feel, or perceive the good, but this is because we still have an idea or concept of what we're labeling as good, and our current experience doesn't fit that definition. This is why we don't immediately understand that whatever is happening is for the good. Seeing everything as good is a practice of full surrender and acceptance. It is initially difficult and can take time to develop.

Rebbe Nachman of Breslov says, "It is the *distance from One* that creates pain." All of the negativity in your life comes as a result of disconnecting and discrediting the Single Source of all happenings. *Distance from One.* This distance gives rise to resistance, and all negativity is resistance in some form or another. We live with a story in our minds about what should and shouldn't be happening. This means something shouldn't have happened in the past, it shouldn't be happening now, or it should happen in the future. This opinionated and biased version of life creates the self-generated life enemies we call "problems." To drop the negativity, we have to drop our version of the story and read a page from the big book of life. There can only be something working against you if you are attached to a desire you can't let go of. Practice and have patience, and life will show you what you need to see with a smile.

EVERYTHING IS FOR THE GOOD.

Seeing the world this way is holy living. Being in the presence of this absolute good while knowing that all is connected with love allows us to celebrate the inner sameness of life, namely the ability to tune into the loving vibration of the universe. The idea that there are two categories, pure and impure, or that we label things as "good and bad," is already a deviation from essential truth, which is all one, all good, and all connected. Holiness is a taste of life precreation. Before we were born, instead of doing, we were being done. We were one with that which surrounded us, took care of us, nurtured us, and gave birth to the miracle of our life. The illusion is that this ended at birth. Our practice is to ignore the negativity. It's an illusion.

But how can you say this when travesties happen in the world?
What do you have to say about tragedy?

I don't.

"And Aharon was silent." The Torah describes Aharon's response to losing two of his children as silence. When discussing tragedy, there is no concept or idea that will ever satisfy the mind. There is no logical explanation that can hold the space for the heartbreak of tragedy. Silence is all there is. The Talmud says that what we stand to gain from going to a house of mourning is the silence. To accept the idea that some things don't fit into our intellect is a gift. It is truly letting go of needing a definitive reason. Reason is of the intellect, and tragedy requires going to a place beyond what words can describe. Try not to answer questions of the heart with answers of the mind. They will only serve to create more pain. Only when the heart is at peace with life can the mind be engaged in the pursuit of deeper ideas.

There is a blessing to be said when apparently good things happen: "Blessed is the Good that continues to bestow good." However, a different blessing is said when there is a loss: "Blessed is the perfect Judge." It's not that there is no blessing; it's that we accept that we can't understand, and so we choose to bless the knowing of something higher and deeper that goes beyond our limitations. Although in the future there will be a time when we can see how everything fits together, as we stand here today, we mourn all loss, we grieve, and we continue to walk our journey.

I understand the value in living a more spiritual life, but I am so busy I can't seem to find time to invest in a spiritual life.

It's not necessarily about changing your schedule as it is about changing your approach to the moments you live. Things might not change on the surface, but internally everything will be different. If it helps, instead of looking at this as living a spiritual life, maybe we could frame it as living a peaceful and joyous life. The way might be one of spirit. Do you have enough time to live a peaceful life? Is there enough time for love? If you are still reading this book, on some level you are already awakened to the ideas it carries. You are ready to live more alive. Appreciate where you are.

Remember that the goal of living life with this perspective is that it allows the true you to shine. Beyond your body and conditioned personality exists a perfect and loving being. This is the truth of who you are. Emmet Fox, in his book *The Ten Commandments*, says it clear and simple: "The yardstick by which we can measure spiritual progress is the degree to which our hearts are filled with unselfish and undemanding love."

CHAPTER NINE

Love, Joy, And Peace

How do you know you are not just kidding yourself and you are really living with Hishtavus?

Love.

Joy.

Peace.

It is really easy to convince yourself that you are somewhere you are not. It's easy to convince yourself that you are experiencing the stillness of equanimity when in fact it is just the ego pretending to be something that looks peaceful. If there isn't positivity radiating from you, peace that you are carrying with you, and a presence of love within, you are not there yet.

When you can smile at someone who accidently walks into you, you are there. When you feel like a calm, grounded force when the house is a wreck, you are there. When you can show love to all people and creatures and show no defensive reactivity, you have arrived.

IT'S ALL THE SAME TO ME.

Do you actually live this way all the time? Do you know anybody who does?

No, and I don't. Except for a very rare few, we have not yet arrived at a time when people can sustain this level of consciousness always and everywhere. However, we are at a growth point. I live with more peace today than I did yesterday. I know many people who live much of the time in this glorious state. It is possible. It is important. And it is for everyone.

Here are a number of different activities that will help support and develop this peace within you:

Spend time in nature. Nature knows no other reality other than peace. Always in full acceptance of what is, nature bends in the ebb and flow of life. The energy that vibrates through your system when you spend time in nature cannot be paralleled in a city. The quiet, the stillness, and the freshness of the outdoors is soothing to the spirit and rejuvenating to the mind.

Study great wisdom. Your mind is a beautiful thing. Fill it with brilliance so it will shine. Fill your mind with spirituality so it takes you to new heights. Basking in the ideas of the great thinkers of this world will train your mind to see greatness, beauty, and creativity everywhere. It opens you up to a deeper dimension, a place where you can flourish.

Find time to enjoy life. This means having fun. Do the things you love to do, not the things that hurt your body. Engage in activities that bring you into the present. Do them alone or with your parents, your siblings, your children, and your friends. If you feel like you would rather be on the beach, go to the beach. If you love to journal, then journal. Listen to the voice inside of you. It is one with who you are.

Live with integrity. Your word is your power. There is no unity in lying or cheating, nor is there joy in surface-level attraction. The more we live by what we know is good in our hearts, the more we can avoid recreating more mental static in our consciousness that reminds us that what we did was inauthentic or wrong. To live in alignment with a deeper truth is not just about having a particular mindset but truly living in harmony with what you know is true.

Spend time alone. An interesting observation is that nearly all great leaders, creators, thinkers, and spiritual guides have come to their greatest revelations when they were alone. There is a stillness and inner silence when you are by yourself, which isn't possible in the noise of the crowd. You might find special gifts showing up at your mental doorstep when you take the time to rest from activity with others.

So if I am always living in a state of having arrived, what am I supposed to do? What about my dreams, ambitions, and goals?

The goal of this book is not to teach you how to play the game but to help you realize there is a game to be played. This means awakening to the dreamlike reality we are in. Until you live in communion with the truth of this reality, you can play the game of life as much as you would like, but you might never arrive at the point of your existence. There is simply so much more to life when it's lived in the context of Hishtavus. When you open up to this truth, you will feel secure and grounded. You can be whomever you like and live the life you truly desire. Walk with the peace of God, and you are free. We all have an outer mission that we cannot avoid. The purpose of this book is to put our sacred and universal inner assignment under the lens of a microscope.

So you ask what of your dreams and aspirations? Go for them. But go with an open mind. Chase your dreams, but chase them with the knowing that there are infinite possibilities about what is truly good for you and those you wish to influence. Do the things you really want to do, knowing that success isn't tied to the outcome you have set in your mind. When you achieve your goals, celebrate them as being part of the Mind of God. Live. Live your life. Live today and tomorrow with the enthusiasm of a child, the passion of lovers, and the wisdom of the sages. You can have it all if you're willing to give it all away.

Fall asleep with a smile, knowing that you are on the right path. This is only the beginning. Remember: the surface is never as important as the depth. But honor, respect, and enjoy the surface, for even the surface is the Kingdom of God.

YOU CAN HAVE IT ALL IF YOU ARE WILLING TO GIVE IT ALL AWAY.

To summarize all we have said: the word *Shaveh* means "the same." There is no better or worse, only different. The difference is only on the surface, and underneath all are the same, equal and one. This perception of sameness is the source of humility. Living in harmony and alignment with God is the foundation of spiritual life. It is the solution to unnecessary drama, negativity, and the creation of our mental stories we label as "problems."

What does sameness do? It is the end of the ego—saying goodbye to what the ego wants and its opinions. We create, sustain, and direct our own pain through our attachment to these fears and desires. We have an opinion about everything and we label things good or bad based on how they make us feel. The self-sacrifice of not allowing our opinion to matter in an absolute way allows the true light of everything to shine through. It's not that nothing matters. No. Everything matters, just not in the way we think it does. It's a practice of letting go of resistance and control. Surrender to what is and allow things to unfold with an inner "yes," accepting the Divine order in our life. You cannot make it work. You can only practice.

Underneath the surface nothing is working against you. There are no opposites. No enemies. Everything happens for a Divine reason that is always *good* in a higher order of reality. A perspective of Oneness and sameness coupled with a deep feeling of love, joy, and peace takes the place of separateness—in the forms of judgment, blame, and criticism. Seen through this lens, all of life's moments become sacred and meaningful.

You know you are there because you radiate peace, love, and joy.

The moment is yours to do with as you wish. This is the true gift. Life is waiting for you to discover who you truly are and what you are doing here. The direction is a good one. The path has been walked before by many others who have led the way.

Let peace be there alongside your journey as you become who you are meant to be. Enjoy the days. Smile with the people around you. Find stillness, be present, and radiate love wherever you go, whomever you're with, and whatever you do. From my spirit to yours, Shalom.

You can only practice. You cannot make it work.

Make it your practice to let go of *making* it work and *allow* it to unfold perfectly.

Resources

The Power of Now: A Guide to Spiritual Enlightenment by Eckhart Tolle; Hodder, London, 2001

The Power of Intention: Learning to Co-create Your World Your Way by Dr. Wayne Dyer; Hay House: Carlsbad, California, 2006

<u>*The Teachings of Don Juan: A Yaqui Way of Knowledge*</u> by Carlos Castaneda; Washington Square Press: New York, New York, 1985

The Four Agreements: A Practical Guide to Personal Freedom (A Toltec Wisdom Book) by Don Miguel Ruiz; Amber-Allen: San Rafael, California, 1997

The Universe Has Your Back: Transform Fear into Faith by Gabrielle Bernstein; Hay House, Carlsbad, California, 2018

A Course in Mysticism and Miracles: Begin Your Spiritual Adventure by Jon Mundy; Red Wheel/Weiser Maine, 2018

The Gifts of Imperfection by Brené Brown; Hazelden Information and Educational Services, Center City, Minnesota, 2010

Resources

You Can be Happy No Matter What: Five Principles for Keeping Life in Perspective by Richard Carslon; New World Library, Novato, California, 2006

Feeling Good: The New Mood Therapy by David Burns; Harper Collins, New York, New York, 1999

A New Earth: Awakening to Your Life's Purpose by Eckhart Tolle; Penguin Putnam Inc, New York, New York, 2005

Emotional Freedom: Liberate Yourself from Negative Emotions and Transform Your Life by Judith Orloff, MD; Random House USA Inc., New York, USA, 2010

The Seat of The Soul by Gary Zukav; Simon and Schuster, New York, New York, 2014

Stillness is the Key: An Ancient Strategy for Modern Life by Ryan Holiday; Profile Books LTD, London, United Kingdom, 2020

A Course in Miracles by Foundation for Inner Peace; Foundation for Inner Peace, Mill Valley, USA, 2008

RESOURCES ON THE SUBJECT OF HISHTAVUS

Psalms 18:8

Sefer Tehillim (ibid) by Rabbi Moshe David Valle; Machon Pitchei Megadim, 1993

Shulchan Aruch, Rama 1:1

Vilna Gaon ibid

Rabbeinu Yona Proverbs 3:6

Tzavas HaRivash Section 5-13 and 145

Keser Shem Tov Section 220

Maharal Chidushei Aggados Shabbos 88b

Bilvavi Mishkan Evneh Book Eight Chapters 6 and 7

Likutai Moharan Torah 51

Meor Einayim Bereishis

Toldos Yaakov Yosef Parshas Chayeh Sarah and Vayechi

Sefas Emes (5)656 dh Bamidrash

Chovos Halevavos Avodas Elokim Chapter 5, Yichud Hamaaseh

Maharsha Brachos 63a dh BaChol

About The Author

After performing for nearly a decade as a popular Los Angeles–based musician, Moshe moved to Jerusalem, where he has spent the last fifteen years immersed in the wellsprings of Talmud, Chassidus, and Kabbalah.

He has devoted his life to seamlessly bridging the worlds of the Torah tradition, mystical wisdom, the true nature of the human mind, and our collective struggles. For years he studied under the guidance of several of the world's premier rabbinical figures and has found a niche for himself sharing his love of life, people, and spirit thro ugh speaking, teaching, and writing. Sensitive and soft-spoken, his care for the people he guides and teaches is palpable.

Find Moshe at www.MosheGersht.com or on his social media platforms:

www.youtube.com/moshegersht

www.instagram.com/moshegersht

www.twitter.com/moshegersht

www.facebook.com/moshegershtofficial

In Loving Memory Of Myriam Venezia Bat Avraham Halevi

In loving memory of Shlomo Ephraim ben Shmuel—Samuel Forest Ozer—a soul who found his inner light and directed it outward to shine upon everyone he met.

In loving memory of Joyce (Bobo) Green

Dedicated to our parents, Rabbi Meilech and Yehudis DuBrow, and Rob and Lise Adatto and to everyone on a journey of personal growth and to those who teach and inspire us on those journeys.

—Ramy and Jazmon DuBrow

In honor and support of our inspiring and dedicated teacher

R' Moshe Gersht

whose guidance, support, and Torah has illuminated our

understanding of ourselves and our world.

The Machon Yaakov Students of 2017–2019

Yoni Belson

Mordechai Bock

Jack Brown

Blake Engelhard

Inbar Goren

Zachary Horwitz

Spencer Isen

Avraham Kovel

Jesse Krumholz

Noah Ohringer

Alex Pearlman

Harael Salkow

Efraim Simkhayev

Kenny Wallach

Ben Weber

Martin Zilberman

Made in the USA
Middletown, DE
09 April 2025

73967744R00092